Canon Andrew White, the vicar of St George's Church in Baghdad, has extensive experience of conflict mediation in Iraq and the wider Middle East. President and CEO of the Foundation for Reconciliation in the Middle East, he has written extensively about conflict resolution and has been involved in many hostage negotiations. He is author of *The Vicar of Baghdad*.

To Dr Malcolm Mathew and his wife Alison

FAITH UNDER FIRE

What the Middle East conflict has taught me about God

Andrew White

MONARCH
BOOKS
Oxford, UK & Grand Rapids, Michigan, USA

First published in the UK in 2011 by Monarch Books
(a publishing imprint of Lion Hudson plc)
Wilkinson House, Jordan Hill Road, Oxford OX2 8DR, England
Tel: +44 (0)1865 302750 Fax: +44 (0)1865 302757
Email: monarch@lionhudson.com

ISBN 978 1 85424 962 3 (print)
ISBN 978 0 85721 094 4 (e-pub)
ISBN 978 0 85721 093 7 (Kindle)
ISBN 978 0 85721 095 1 (pdf)

Reprinted 2011 (three times).

Distributed by:
UK: Marston Book Services, PO Box 269, Abingdon, Oxon, OX14 4YN
USA: Kregel Publications, PO Box 2607, Grand Rapids, Michigan 49501

The text paper used in this book has been made from wood independently
certified as having come from sustainable forests.

British Library Cataloguing Data
A catalogue record for this book is available from the British Library

Printed and bound in the UK by MPG Books.

CONTENTS

1

MY PREVIOUS LIFE

There is really very little resemblance between my present life and the life I thought I would be living now. I began my adult life as a student at St Thomas' Hospital, London, studying surgery and anaesthetics, and went on to become an operating department practitioner. I assumed I would continue to pursue a career in medicine, but God had other plans. The world I occupied then is completely different to the one I occupy now, but nevertheless I learned some valuable lessons – not least the ability to react quickly in situations. When a patient goes into cardiac arrest you have to react immediately. When someone points a gun at you, intending to pull the trigger, you must also react immediately. If you have to think about dodging a bullet, it has already hit you. On the streets of Baghdad, my medical training has probably been more use to me than my theological training at Cambridge.

It was while working and training at St Thomas' that God called me and set me on the path that eventually led me to Iraq. One night I was on call to deal with any cardiac emergencies as part of the hospital's Crash Team and stepped outside for a while to get some fresh air and to pray in the hospital grounds. I looked across the River Thames towards Big Ben on the opposite bank. I was thrilled to be at St Thomas' and I remember thanking the Almighty that I had successfully completed my training. I was fortunate to be doing the very thing I had always wanted to do in the very hospital where I had always wanted to work. I asked God what should be the next step in my life. Like a thunderbolt the answer came to me, but it wasn't the one I was expecting. I felt very strongly that He wanted me to offer myself for service in the Church of England.

Remarkably, as a child of ten I had said that I wanted to be an anaesthetist and a priest. But that was then and this was now. I no longer wanted to be a priest; I was enjoying my work at St Thomas' too much to give it up. Yet I knew, without a doubt, that God had spoken to me. For a few hours I struggled with His words, but eventually gave in and decided that obeying His will would be best. As I did, I was immediately aware of the presence and glory of God in a way I had never known before. As I returned to the operating theatre in the early hours of the morning, the Lord was there. When my shift ended and I went home, God was there also. He was at St Mark's, Kennington, where I went to church, in the Christian Union at work and at my home group. I felt so acutely aware of God's presence all the time, in fact, that I must have appeared rather strange to my friends. A few of them told me as much!

One friend who accepted me as I was, however, and never ceased to encourage me was Malcolm Mathew. We spent a lot of time together. Malcolm looked out for me, on one occasion coming to the hospital and forcing me to go home with him, knowing I had worked for forty-five hours straight without a break! Each Sunday he and I would take patients to the hospital chapel and afterwards we would go on to Speakers' Corner in Hyde Park, where I would take my turn to preach. It was a fertile training ground for later in life when I would frequently be called upon to speak in public.

More than twenty years later Malcolm is a consultant anaesthetist at King's College Hospital in London. He is still a member of the Territorial Army, as he was back then, and has often been in Iraq at the same time as me. Malcolm and his wife, Alison, are godparents to our eldest son, Josiah, and he remains one of my closest and longest-standing friends in life. Added to this, Alison and my wife, Caroline, are the closest of friends. Our friendship has been a double blessing: I have a friend who understands what it means to live out one's faith under fire – and we each have a wife who knows what it means to have a husband with such a calling.

Fulfilled ambition

Whilst continuing to work at St Thomas', I commenced a long, slow journey towards ordination. Eventually I attended a selection conference to see if I was the right type of person to be trained for ordination, and I was selected and offered a place at Ridley Hall, Cambridge, to study theology.

I began to prepare studiously for this next step. I remember trying to learn Greek while still working at the hospital! In the end I decided to take a few months' break before moving to Cambridge, intending to spend some time praying in a monastery, but first I wanted to visit the Kingdom Faith Bible

Week to hear Colin Urquhart speak. Colin, himself a former Anglican priest, had made a significant impact on the life of St Mark's, Kennington. I volunteered to serve in the clinic on site where several thousand people would be camping. I had a wonderful week there and our team saw a number of miracles take place in the clinic. It was an inspiring experience and I looked forward to what God might do next.

But for all my excitement about moving into training for ordination, I had one regret, perhaps better described as an unfulfilled ambition. I had not managed to achieve the one thing I had always wanted to do at St Thomas' – to run the Crash Team. I had been called to assist them on many occasions, and had even volunteered for unpaid duties to gain more experience, but it was my ambition one day to head up the team. God, in His graciousness, decided to lend me a hand.

This was in the days before mobile phones. I remember calling home to speak to my mother, as I usually did, and she sounded frantic. She told me she had been desperately trying to get in contact with me for two days. When I asked why, she told me that St Thomas' Hospital had been trying to call me and urgently wanted me to contact them. When I called the hospital I discovered, to my astonishment, that they were having some serious problems in the cardiac emergency unit and had been forced to suspend most of the Crash Team. They asked if I would be willing to come back and run the team until they were able to resolve the problem. I didn't need to think about it – I said yes immediately. I was being given the chance to fulfil my ambition! I returned to St Thomas' for several months and experienced the most wonderful days of my entire medical career.

I ran the Crash Team right up until the day before I was due to begin my studies at Cambridge. The next day my life changed radically. I went from the hospital corridors, where my day was spent literally running from one crisis to the next, to the corridors of learning where I was engaged in studying and more studying! At first I felt very much out of my depth. Previously I had known what I was doing and I was good at my job. Now I suddenly felt very unskilled. Worse than that, before I had enjoyed a constant awareness of God's presence. Now I felt as though I had stepped into a spiritual desert. From this point on God seemed strangely remote – not only to me but to many of my fellow students. This is not an uncommon experience. My friend and fellow canon, J. John, told me that for him seminary was more like a cemetery! For many, theological training involved periods of real doubt. I thank God that, despite my difficulties, doubt was never something I experienced then (or at any time, for that matter).

An unexpected turn

Despite my training at Cambridge being mentally and spiritually taxing, I was still enjoying my time there. It challenged me to think deeply about many issues I had previously dismissed as irrelevant and it ultimately taught me that when God seems distant, He is actually very near. But in my second year a new challenge presented itself. I became very unwell, noticing that my coordination was bad, and I frequently felt dreadful. My energy levels were constantly low and I developed serious neurological symptoms. I was eventually admitted to Addenbrooke's Hospital in Cambridge, but after a short time there and several examinations the doctors told me there was nothing wrong with me. I'm not sure how they reached this conclusion, as I left the hospital barely able to walk! But I was taken back to Ridley Hall and cared for in the Principal's Lodge. After several days I was taken home to my parents' house where I was confined to bed until the next term began three months later.

I returned to Cambridge to recommence my studies, but still felt ill and worked from my bed much of the time. In order to attend lectures I had to be wheeled around in a wheelchair. But I was determined to keep studying, despite these difficulties. I continued to be observed by my doctors and was eventually diagnosed with myalgic encephalitis (ME), also known as "chronic fatigue syndrome".

In all I spent four years at Cambridge, with part of it spent in Jerusalem studying Judaism. Apart from one period of twelve months when I was too ill to do anything, I would return to St Thomas' during my vacations and work there. I was paid locum rates for this work, which meant I earned as much in one year as I would have done if I'd been working there full time. I often thought I must be the best-paid student in the country!

It was during my time at Cambridge that the foundations for my later work in the Middle East were laid. Judaism became my main area of interest. I studied under Professor Nicholas de Lange. He was not only a Hebraic scholar but also a Reform (modern) Rabbi. To this day I consider him to be the most significant and influential lecturer I had at Cambridge. I also began visiting the Orthodox Synagogue in Cambridge, where I learned a great deal – not least the Orthodox Jewish ways of worship, interwoven with centuries-old prayers. At no time did I feel that my own faith was challenged in any way; in fact it just grew stronger.

My journey into reconciliation

Then an event occurred that would be pivotal in shaping the rest of my life. The university's Christian Union (CICCU) was holding its major triennial mission and it decided to invite Jews for Jesus, a major evangelical organization that targeted Jews, to take part. The university's Jewish students were in uproar – so much so that one Jewish newspaper in London ran the headline, "Holy War in Cambridge". Since I was the only Christian anyone knew who went to both the Synagogue and the Jewish Society, as well as the Christian Union, I was asked to mediate. I didn't realize it at the time, but God was positioning me for a particular service to Him and this was the beginning of a lifelong ministry of reconciliation. I spent many hours discussing the issues with both CICCU and the Jewish Society. It helped me understand that, above all else, people in conflict need to learn to listen to each other. In the end there was no compromise offered from either side and the event still went ahead, but subsequently I and some other students formed a society called Cambridge University Jews and Christians (CUJAC) in an effort to encourage peace and mutual understanding. I was appointed as its first President and within a short while the society became a major force for reconciliation between Jews and Christians.

I was amazed at how God took this small step of faith and expanded it into something much larger. As CUJAC's first President, I found myself playing an increasing role in reconciliation in the UK and beyond. Three people were significant in my life at this time and instrumental during these early stages. Paul Mendel, who at the time was Deputy Director of the Council of Christians and Jews (CCJ), was a great adviser and became a good friend. With his assistance CUJAC was soon a branch of CCJ. Then there was Sir Sigmund Sternberg, who was a member of the CCJ committee, but also the Chair of the International Council of Christians and Jews (ICCJ). The third person was Dr Elisabeth Maxwell, a great scholar of Jewish–Christian relations and the wife of Robert Maxwell, the infamous owner of Mirror Group Newspapers. Throughout the rest of my student days in Cambridge these people remained very important to me.

It was not long before Sir Sigmund got me involved with the work of ICCJ. Headquartered in Germany, this was the body that brought together all the national branches of CCJ from around the world, and it wielded considerable influence. Every year ICCJ held a major international conference hosted by a different nation and this was always preceded by a conference for its Young Leadership Section (YLS), geared towards those under thirty-five years of age. I remember receiving a desperate phone call only a matter of weeks before this conference, asking me if I would help to organize it – even though I had never been to one before! I agreed and ended up organizing almost everything. There were representatives from more than twenty countries. Near to the end of the conference there was the usual annual general meeting which elected the board of the YLS. I decided to put myself forward as a candidate and, to my surprise, I was not just elected to the board but invited to be its President. It was a position that afforded me a lot of influence and proved to be significant during the early years of my ordained life, since I didn't hold the post just for one year (like most of my predecessors) but was re-elected each year for five years.

"Take risks, not care"

When I first went to Israel in 1988 my expenses were paid by two further people who became friends: the late Duke of Devonshire, who was the patron of CUJAC, and the Jewish philanthropist Sidney Corob CBE. Both were deeply involved in Jewish–Christian relations and both became very important to me. Between them they not only paid for all my studies in Jerusalem (at the Hebrew University and then at an Ultra-Orthodox Jewish seminary) but all my subsequent visits to Israel as well. I found it strange that a young seminarian like me should become so familiar with the great and the good.

It was an invitation from Sidney Corob to a function at one of his bases in Mayfair that led to my first meeting with the man who would become my mentor in life: Lord Donald Coggan, the former Archbishop of Canterbury and the President of the ICCJ. I had heard him lecture many times, but had never met him personally. We immediately became friends. At the time I had no idea just how significant he would become to me. As we left the meeting that day, I walked down the road a little way with him before saying goodbye. As we parted he hugged me warmly (as was his custom) and said the words that would become my motto in life: "Don't take care, take risks." That phrase embedded itself in my spirit and I have sought to follow his advice ever since.

Because of my ill health, my time at Cambridge was extended by one year so that I could complete my studies. Increasingly I spent my time studying in Israel, paid for by my friends. My time in Jerusalem added to the foundations already laid for what was to come. I learned a great deal about Judaism and indeed the Hebrew language, and also realized I needed to learn about Eastern Christianity and Islam – a journey that continues to this day. One day, my ultra-Orthodox rabbi told me I needed to go and meet a certain lady. It surprised me that such a conservative rabbi should tell me to go and meet with a woman – that was unusual in itself – but even more surprising was the fact that she was a Christian who led a worship centre based in her home in East Jerusalem. I attended one of her services and it was unlike anything I'd experienced before. I could only describe her as being very large and very Pentecostal! Her name was Ruth Heflin and I have often since referred to her as the most frightening woman I've ever met.

Ruth preached powerfully and loudly, and sang a lot. I was slightly puzzled as to why the rabbi thought I should meet her, but God used her to speak into my life. At the end of the service Ruth singled me out and began prophesying over me. She said that my calling was to work for peace in the Middle East. At the time I presumed that this meant a life spent in Israel. In the years that followed, when I was working there, I often recalled her words and knew that they had been fulfilled. Now that I am based in Iraq much of the time, I think about her words even more. I only met Ruth three times in total, but each time God used her to impact my life powerfully.

When I returned to England it was time to look for a parish in which to serve my curacy. My health continued to be problematic and although I was able to function – just – I experienced many ups and downs. The Bishop of Southwark, Ronald Bowlby, and his suffragan in Kingston, Peter Selby, were both very supportive. Bishop Peter very much wanted me to go to St Mark's, Battersea Rise. Though they raised serious questions about my health during my interview there, I was eventually offered the job. I left Cambridge in June 1990, returned to Jerusalem for a couple of months, and was ordained at the end of September that year in Southwark Cathedral. I greatly enjoyed my three-year curacy and learned much from the vicar, Paul Perkin, about how to run a church in a professional manner and get things done. Friday was my day off, in theory, but I frequently returned to St Thomas' on a voluntary basis to work as an assistant in Anaesthetics. I didn't imagine there were many curates doing anaesthetics on the side! I have never been one for taking much time off.

In addition to my various duties as a curate I continued to fulfil many diverse duties in the ICCJ. As well as making trips to the ICCJ's headquarters in Heppenheim, Germany, to spend time with Lord Coggan, I also visited CCJ bases in a number of other countries and was even granted regular audiences with Pope John Paul II, as in 1993 the Vatican was preparing to begin the process of recognizing the State of Israel. I admired the Pope and he became a genuine friend. Looking back on my curacy, I am acutely aware of the graciousness of my vicar, Paul Perkin. Few vicars would have allowed their curates to do the things I did!

It was near the end of my first year at St Mark's, while I

was preaching at the Sunday evening service, that I spotted someone from the pulpit I had not seen before. She was young and beautiful, and I confess that in the midst of my sermon I thought, "I like what I see!" After the service I went and talked to her. She told me she had just moved to St Mark's from a church in the City of London. At the time I was busy organizing a mission at the church with J. John, so I asked her if she would like to help. I didn't really know anything about her, but this would give me an excuse to meet with her again! I was delighted when she agreed. I soon discovered that her name was Caroline and that she was a lawyer in the City. In a matter of days we fell in love with each other and began a relationship.

The next step

Just six weeks later I took Caroline to Cambridge and we went punting on the Cam. Somewhere between Clare College and King's I asked her to marry me. I had decided several years before that if I ever proposed to anyone, it would be at that very spot. Being a lawyer, Caroline's immediate response was, "Maybe"! But a few moments later she said "Yes", and from the end of the punt I threw her the ring I'd had made for her. Later we travelled down to Hampshire to visit her family so I could ask her father's permission for us to get married. He agreed, though he commented that it was happening much sooner than he'd expected. Ten months later we were married by Lord Coggan in a remote little church near the farm where Caroline grew up. We spent part of our honeymoon in the Golan Heights and part of it in Jerusalem, where I arranged a party so that Caroline could meet all my friends. We had no idea what our life together would be like. Already involved intimately in inter-religious affairs, I had every intention of maintaining this "interest", but assumed my life would primarily be spent as a cleric back in England.

Marriage has a way of exposing a person's true nature and I soon learned that I was quite a strange, even difficult, person. I well remember one day getting annoyed and telling Caroline that she was cutting the carrots wrong. I told her that in our house we always cut them lengthways! Fortunately, the woman I married is a wonderful person and utterly patient. Instead of becoming irritated by my idiosyncrasies, she was always understanding and willing to teach me how to improve my odd ways! Many years later she continues to do so.

Towards the end of my curacy, in 1993, my archdeacon, David Gerrard, suggested I should put myself forward for a position at a nearby church in Clapham: the Church of the Ascension, Balham Hill. The congregation there was seriously dwindling and the idea was to do a church plant or "graft" with people coming from St Mark's, Battersea and Holy Trinity, Brompton to inject fresh life and energy. One other person being considered for the role was the curate of John Sentamu, the current Archbishop of York, who at the time was a vicar in nearby Tulse Hill. I was offered the job and soon Caroline and I were moving a mile up the road to the biggest vicarage I had ever seen.

The new church was a real challenge. We were introducing a group of around fifty young professional people into a small congregation consisting mainly of elderly, working-class and black people. But at the same time it was a wonderful experience and I loved the people there. It provided me with another opportunity to hone my skills as a reconciler. Our worship was very broad: we always started Sunday morning with a traditional Anglican Eucharist, while in the evening the service was informal and very much in the charismatic tradition. Despite the very different focus of each service, we enjoyed great unity. The church grew and I became involved in every aspect of community life, from community centres to local schools to local politics, often finding myself being a member of or chairing committees.

I continued to be very involved with Jewish–Christian relations and travelled internationally to engage with various religious leaders on behalf of the ICCJ, increasingly working closely with the Vatican. I continued to meet regularly with Pope John Paul II and managed to take Caroline to meet him on one occasion. In August 1996 our first child, Josiah, was born. I was delighted that he was delivered at St Thomas' Hospital where I had trained and worked. Josiah was baptized in early December by Lord Coggan in a truly wonderful, memorable service.

During this time my involvement with the local council increased. Council-related meetings would often be held in our vicarage and eventually I was asked if I would stand for Wandsworth Council. I discussed the matter at length with our church leaders. The great majority, though not all, were in favour of me standing. In fact, most people locally seemed to approve of the idea of their vicar standing for elected office. Polling day arrived and I did a little canvassing in the evening before going to the town hall to wait for the results. To be perfectly honest, I wasn't that bothered whether I won or not – but my pile of votes got bigger and bigger and when the final results were announced, I had won my council seat with a very large majority.

The ward included my parish and two others. I had to make it clear to everyone that in these other parishes I was only concerned with council and not church work. I was given specific responsibility for social services and quickly discovered that much of politics has to do with making compromises. There were many times when I disagreed with decisions that were being made. On one occasion I felt so passionately about an issue I was voting against that I told my colleagues I would be forced to resign from my role of leading social services. On that occasion the decision was reversed and I remained.

There are big differences between local and central government, but many principles can be transferred from one to the other. Little did I know how useful this experience would prove to be in the future. Not least, I learned a great deal about how to maintain your faith in the face of opposition and how to be led by the Holy Spirit through the metaphorical fire. God was preparing me for the next phase of my life.

WHY GO INTO THE FIRE?

I will never forget that day. I was sitting at my desk in my study when the phone rang. I answered and it was our diocesan bishop in Southwark, Roy Williamson. Roy had heard that a key job relating to international affairs and reconciliation had become available – the post of Director of International Ministry for the diocese and cathedral of Coventry. It was a very significant, high-profile role. The outgoing leader, Paul Oestreicher, had established the centre as a force for good throughout the world. The post also included a residentiary canonry at the cathedral. The bishop thought I should apply for the job.

It was clear from the job description that my life and work to date had positioned and equipped me well for such a task. My role with the ICCJ had seen me promoting dialogue between the three great monotheistic faiths, and I had travelled to nations such as Kenya and Nigeria where there were increasing tensions between Christians and Muslims. In Kenya, especially, I had spent time listening to both communities and eventually, after a long and difficult process,

I had persuaded both parties to listen to each other.

I faced several problems, however, in applying for this job. First, at just thirty-three years of age I was considered a little too young and had not been ordained long enough to hold such a senior position in the Church of England. Second, I had no desire to leave my parish in London and certainly did not wish to move north to the Midlands. Lastly, I felt I could not simply abandon the position to which I'd been elected on Wandsworth Council. I prayed much about the issue but did not receive any clear direction, so eventually I decided the best thing to do was to apply for the post and leave the outcome to God.

A few days later I was surprised to be informed that I had been short-listed for the position. Since I had never been to Coventry or seen its two cathedrals, I decided to visit the city prior to my interview. I confess, I was totally overwhelmed by what I saw. I had never witnessed such a powerful symbol of reconciliation. The fourteenth-century cathedral (which until 1918 had been only a very large parish church) lay in ruins, all but destroyed by German bombs on the night of 14 November 1940. Standing right next to it was the new cathedral – awesome, imposing and full of the presence of the Almighty. The following day was Sunday, so I attended the main morning worship service. To say it was inspirational would be an understatement! It was Lent and the choir processed through the building, singing the litany. The Provost at the time, John Petty, welcomed me warmly, not knowing who I was. By the end of the service I was utterly convinced that this was the place where God wanted me to be.

Shortly after this visit I went before the interview panel,

chaired by Colin Bennetts, who was making his first senior appointment after becoming diocesan Bishop. Afterwards I returned to London and two days later Colin phoned me to say he wished to appoint me to the position. I had already discussed the matter in depth with Caroline. We were both convinced that we had been called to this ministry together and had already resolved to do whatever God asked us to do – so I accepted without hesitation. We were willingly walking into the "fire" – a place of great conflict, but also one of great joy and hope. We were willing to embrace whatever God had for us – though at the time we had no idea just how hot it would become.

I then faced the difficult task of informing our Balham Hill congregation that we were leaving to move to Coventry. I loved these people very much and had assumed we would be together for a long time. I picked my moment and, at the end of a service, broke the news. It was one of the most difficult speeches I had ever had to give in public and I couldn't hold back the tears. It became very clear to me that not everything God calls us to do is painless. Nevertheless, we prepared ourselves for the move. Caroline was now pregnant with our second child, so the relocation process was more challenging than ever.

When we finally arrived in Coventry it was clear that life there would be very different. We made one last visit to Balham Hill for a final service and farewell, and the congregation gave us an incredible send-off I will never forget. The following week I was installed in Coventry Cathedral. Many friends and colleagues from London attended, including the Mayor of Wandsworth and several other councillors. I had decided to hold on to my seat on the council until I had completed my term – a decision that proved to be contentious. At the time, Wandsworth Council were initiating some major cuts to social service funding. Some of those opposed to the changes also came up to Coventry to protest and handed out leaflets to all and sundry which demanded that the council "Fire the Canon!" It must have been clear to my new colleagues that the man who was replacing the sometimes controversial Paul Oestreicher was not without controversy himself!

A day of tragedy and splendour

Next, the real work began. Apart from running the International Ministry for the diocese and cathedral, I was also responsible for directing the International Centre for Reconciliation (ICR). The ICR was a highly significant ministry that was a focal point for reconciliation throughout the world. To date, much of its work had been connected to Eastern Europe and Germany, but I could see that our main focus would increasingly need to shift towards the Islamic world. The previous year had seen the collapse of communism throughout much of the old Soviet bloc, in Poland, Hungary, East Germany, Bulgaria, Czechoslovakia and Romania, and it was evident now that the axis of tension in the years ahead was going to be the Islamic world and the Middle East. In particular, I believed that we needed to concentrate on Israel, Palestine and Iraq. The former I knew well, but I had yet to visit Iraq.

Meanwhile my workload was demanding. I needed to visit Wandsworth regularly on council business, while at the same time getting to grips with my new role, and it wasn't easy splitting life between the two. I had only been in office a few weeks, however, when my balance and vision began to deteriorate seriously. It quickly got to the point where I felt I must visit my doctor, and when I did I was admitted to hospital that same day and remained there for the next five weeks. One afternoon a doctor came to inform me that I had multiple sclerosis. It was devastating news. That very afternoon Caroline went into labour and was admitted to the same hospital. That evening I was taken by wheelchair to the delivery suite and witnessed the birth of my second son, Jacob. I have often since described that day as one of both tragedy and splendour. In many ways it was indicative of all that was to follow, my life frequently swinging between grief and exhilaration. Let me say, however, that I did not question God that day – and have not since – about why I contracted this incurable disease. My medical training had taught me that there are simply no answers to the "Why me?" questions we always tend to ask.

My colleagues rightly wondered whether I would ever be able to do my job which, of course, included a great deal of travelling, but after leaving hospital I was soon back at my desk and pursuing my work with vigour. My overseas commitments fell into two categories. First, the ICR had established a network of what are called "Cross of Nails" centres around the world, particularly in the USA and Germany. (Coventry is twinned with Dresden – as it is with Volgograd [formerly Stalingrad] and many other cities and towns.) At that time there were over 250 such centres and my role involved visiting each of them in due course. Second, there would need to be increased visits to the Middle East as we shifted our focus and pursued reconciliation work there.

The ICR had been conceived in the depths of the Second World War when Dick Howard, the provost of Coventry Cathedral, made a commitment on the day after its destruction by the Luftwaffe to seek reconciliation rather than revenge. Famously, he wrote in chalk on the wall of the ruined sanctuary just two words: "Father, forgive". Six weeks later, on Christmas Day 1940, he announced on national radio that once the War was over he would work with Britain's former enemies "to build a kinder, more Christ-like world". Today, Coventry is known as "the City of Peace and Reconciliation".

I was only the fourth director of the ICR, and the first to have been born since the end of the War. Indeed, I was not alive when Coventry's new cathedral was consecrated in 1963! My predecessor, Paul Oestreicher, was very different from me, though I really respected him. He was very left-wing politically and very liberal theologically, whereas I was very conservative in both respects. As a German-born Jew whose family had escaped the Holocaust by fleeing to New Zealand in 1939, he had been extremely active in working to heal wounds in Eastern Europe after the War, long before he came to Coventry. He was also deeply involved in South Africa and was a friend of Desmond Tutu.

Two major things we had in common were our deep loves for Judaism and for those people who are seen as outsiders. Both of us were willing to work with those whom most people thought were too bad to deal with. Paul had enormous experience in this area and I learned much from him. He had spent a huge amount of time working behind the Iron Curtain and, like me, regularly took risks to fix broken relationships. It became clear to me that there is never one, unequivocal way to bring about reconciliation. Every situation requires a different approach. However, there are certain essentials:

* The person seeking to bring about reconciliation has to have a real relationship with all sides and has to listen to their concerns.
* Eventually, the two sides in the conflict have to meet.
* Each side must be willing to listen to the other and be willing to make compromises.
* Any resolution to the conflict has to offer something to both sides.
* Once a resolution has been agreed, the two sides must spend time with each other.
* The whole process needs to be steeped in prayer.

The road to Iraq

It was obvious to me in 1998 that a major obstacle to peace around the world was the conflict between the Israelis and the Palestinians. Previously I had met the Syrian Orthodox archbishop Mar Severios and longed to visit his homeland, since a rapprochement with Syria seemed to me to be crucial to the whole Middle East Peace Process. But, unfortunately, to do so proved impossible. During one meeting with Mar Severios we decided that I should travel with him to Damascus to visit the patriarch of his church, Mar Ignatius Zakka I. But after driving across the desert from Jordan we were stopped at the border and I was refused entry. When I asked why, the border guards responded, "You may be a man of God but have you just landed from heaven? We know you have been in Israel!" I have tried many times since to get into Syria, but even though I have two different passports, one for Israel and one for Arab countries, I have never been allowed in. The only other country to which I have been refused entry is Iran. As far as the Iranians are concerned, I am a friend of Israel and so cannot be a friend to them. Oh, how desperately there needs to be a restoration of relations between Iran and the West! I hope one day to be able to be involved there, not least because of the excellent relationships I have with the Shia clerics in Iraq.

I have told much of the story of my work for peace in Israel/Palestine in *The Vicar of Baghdad*.[1] Our most significant achievement there was the Alexandria Declaration (or "the First Alexandria Declaration of the Religious Leaders of the Holy Land") in 2002, in which Jewish, Christian and Muslim leaders joined in calling on "followers of the divine religions" to respect the sanctity of the Holy Land and not to allow bloodshed to pollute it. I organized the whole process, which was chaired by Dr George (later Lord) Carey, then the Archbishop of Canterbury. (He and his wife, Eileen, became very close friends of mine, and it was with him that I set up the Foundation for Relief and Reconciliation in the Middle East in 2005 when the time came for me to leave the ICR.) The declaration was endorsed by both the Israeli prime minister, Ariel Sharon, and the president of Egypt, Hosni Mubarak. Sadly, this work has not progressed well since then, although some of the people who were present at Alexandria have been able to achieve something at grass-roots level.

---

1   Monarch, 2009.

People often ask me why I am not still involved in Israel/ Palestine. It is true that after the liberation of Iraq the new Archbishop of Canterbury, Dr Rowan Williams, asked me to concentrate my efforts there. But peacemaking is all about relationships with people who can make a difference, and the key people I had been working with in Israel/Palestine are no longer active. I have never had the same relationship with Dr Williams that I had with Dr Carey, not least because Dr Williams spoke out so strongly against war in 2003. Yasser Arafat, to whom I was so close, died in 2004. Ariel Sharon suffered a stroke in 2006 and is now in a coma. My closest colleague, Rabbi Michael Melchior, lost his position in the Israeli government in 2006 and his seat in the Knesset in 2009. Of course, I have many other contacts in Israel/Palestine, but funding for my work there, from both the Foreign Office and private donors, dried up in 2007, and in the meantime I had become ever more involved in Iraq – as the vicar of St George's, Baghdad, in particular. However, now that Barack Obama has revived the Middle East Peace Process, funding may become available again. And now that St George's lay pastor, Faiz, has finally been ordained, I may soon have the time to return to Israel/Palestine. I certainly hope so – I love that land and its peoples!

I have told the story of my involvement in Iraq at some length in two of my books, *Iraq: Searching for Hope*[2] and *The Vicar of Baghdad*, but perhaps I should mention why I felt I ought to get involved there. Israel/Palestine I knew well and Paul Oestreicher had already done some work there; there were Cross of Nails centres in Jerusalem and Galilee. But Iraq

---

2   Continuum, 2005, 2007.

was a different matter. Nobody from Coventry had been there, though the ICR had played an important role in supporting the families and friends of British people who had been taken as hostages or "human shields" by the Iraqi state in 1990 in the build-up to the Gulf War of 1991. Now there was widespread concern for the Iraqi people who were suffering greatly under the sanctions imposed by the United Nations. Then, in 1998, the Americans and the British launched a relentless three-day attack on Baghdad with bombs and cruise missiles, as a result of an ongoing dispute over the access given to UN weapons inspectors in Iraq. The onslaught was so dreadful that people still talk about it today. As a result of this, many in Iraq were urging me to visit to assess the impact of these events on the lives of ordinary people, and to see whether there was anything I could do to work towards brokering a reconciliation between Saddam Hussein's regime and the West.

Most of the Muslims I met, whether Shia or Sunni, were distressed by the suffering that was being caused by the sanctions (though this was not always true of the many Iraqi refugees I had got to know in Britain), and even Yasser Arafat asked me once, "Will you do something?" The issues were geopolitical, going back to Iraq's invasion and annexation of Kuwait in 1990, but there were many throughout the Islamic world who saw the conflict essentially as a matter of Christians attacking Muslims. I thought it was important to show that this was not the case, and that there were many Christians who were very sympathetic to Muslims and, especially, who cared about the Iraqi people. If I could, I also wanted to try to engage with the political leaders on both sides.

But it was not easy to gain entry into Iraq. I tried to obtain a visa through every official channel I knew of, but failed. I was told at every stage that if I wanted to do something to help Iraq, I should just work towards removing the sanctions. Eventually, amidst much frustration, I gathered my staff at the cathedral and we prayed fervently together. The late Archbishop of Canterbury William Temple once said, "When you pray about something, coincidences happen. When you don't, they don't." To prove this point, after we had prayed earnestly, the very next day I received, out of the blue, a personal invitation from Tariq Aziz, then Iraq's deputy prime minister, to visit him in Baghdad. Arrangements were made and in a matter of days I was on my way. Flying into the country was out of the question and so plans were made for me to drive the fourteen hours to Baghdad from Amman in Jordan. The BBC asked me to take a tape recorder with me so that they could make a radio programme about my visit. This was the first of many visits to "the land between the two rivers".

I will never forget that first visit to Iraq. It was an arduous journey – the desert roads from Jordan were not good – and no staff accompanied me, so I had no one to talk to. Having reached border control and passed into the country, I was ushered into a kind of "VIP lounge", though I could scarcely imagine a worse-looking place. The state of the toilets was unmentionable and there was a strange "duty free" counter where, amongst other things, an odd-looking, rusty frying pan was on sale. (Five years later, just before the 2003 war, I noticed that the frying pan was still there!) I sat in this "lounge" for over two hours, waiting for my visa to be stamped, though there was no queue of people. Visiting Iraq wasn't exactly popular then.

The roads in Iraq were considerably better than those in Jordan. We travelled at 140 kilometres per hour for what seemed like a long time. Arriving on the outskirts of Baghdad, the first thing that struck me was the number of cars with broken windscreens. I asked my driver why this was and he told me it was because of the sanctions: people simply could not buy replacement windscreens – one of the many items that were currently not allowed into Iraq.

Shortly, we arrived at al-Rashid – the "official" hotel of the Iraqi government. On entering, I was surprised to see on the floor a large tiled mosaic of President George Bush Senior. Underneath, written in both English and Arabic were the words, "Bush is criminal". The process of checking in was very slow – something I would become accustomed to in years to come. Meanwhile, security was extremely tight and I was surrounded by police and soldiers, all bearing arms.

I was approached by a man who said he was from the Ministry of Protocol and would accompany me throughout my stay. I was soon to learn that he was in fact a member of the Mukhabarat (the Iraqi Intelligence Service), sent to spy on me and record my every word and action.

When the day arrived for me to meet with Tariq Aziz, the Mukhabarat's presence increased considerably, as did the number of police. It was obvious that everyone was nervous about this meeting. Eventually I was ushered in to meet Tariq Aziz – the first of numerous meetings – and our time together was very cordial. At the end he asked me if I would visit again, bringing other church leaders with me. I said I would and we departed on very friendly terms. As I left his office I became acutely aware that I had entered into the line of fire, but now

I was committed – it was up to God to bring whatever He wanted out of this relationship.

I was conscious of the need to get to know other key political and religious leaders in Iraq. It proved to be a long and complex process – not least because, for the first time in my life, I was trying to form relationships with people some of whom had sanctioned torture and mass murder. At first, I have to confess, I was rather naive and often did not realize that what I was being told was simply propaganda – so that I would make the right noises whenever I was interviewed on Iraqi TV. It took several visits before it struck me that everybody was telling me exactly the same thing: that the effects of the sanctions were dreadful, that the effects of the depleted uranium in the nation were disastrous, and that Saddam was wonderful. Eventually, I realized that people were saying these things because they had no choice. Wherever I went the Mukhabarat was watching and listening. I had spent hours talking to Tariq Aziz and other government ministers, but now saw that even these men were not really free. The more time I spent in Iraq, the more I appreciated how evil the regime actually was. And when I had dinner with Saddam's two odious sons – at their insistence – they thanked me for all I was doing!

Nonetheless, as I look back, I can see how crucial my efforts were to what I am doing now. I was able to form substantive relationships with some key religious leaders. My befriending of Ayatollah (now Grand Ayatollah) Hussein al-Sadr and Sheikh Dr Abdel Latif Humayem, which may have seemed rather inconsequential to most people in the run-up to the invasion, has since turned out to be enormously important in ways that no one back then expected. Moreover, if I had not visited Iraq before the war I would now be viewed merely as an accessory of the Coalition. The fact that I did so means that my concern for and commitment to the Iraqi people have been recognized as real and enduring. On the other hand, with the exception of a few journalists, none of the British people I encountered in Iraq before its liberation, who were opposing both the sanctions and the invasion, have I ever seen there since!

Over the next three years I visited Iraq regularly, trying unsuccessfully to work at reconciliation whilst, at the same time, working at relief efforts and seeing some progress. Then the day happened that we will never forget: 9/11. I was sitting in my study at Coventry Cathedral, preparing to return to Iraq the next day, when the news started to come through of the planes crashing into the Twin Towers and the Pentagon.

It was a devastating blow. I knew that life would never be the same again. I hoped that somehow the Lord would come into this tragedy. I found it difficult to know how to pray, so I left my study and went and stood in the neighbouring ruins of the old cathedral. I prayed the Coventry Litany of Reconciliation and all the staff joined in:

All have sinned and fallen short of the glory of God.
The hatred which divides nation from nation, race from race, class from class
Father Forgive.
The covetous desires of people and nations to possess what is not their own
Father Forgive.

*The greed which exploits the work of human
hands and lays waste the earth
Father Forgive.
Our envy of the welfare and happiness of others,
Father Forgive.
Our indifference to the plight of the imprisoned,
the homeless, the refugee,
Father Forgive.
The lust which dishonours the bodies of men,
women and children,
Father Forgive.
The pride which leads us to trust in ourselves and
not in God,
Father Forgive.
Be kind to one another, tender-hearted, forgiving
one another, as God in Christ forgave you.*

Further preparation for the fire

By the following year, 2002, my focus in Iraq had become clearer. I had asked God to show me how to relieve the suffering of the many people I had grown to love, and the ICR became involved in various humanitarian projects, including helping to set up the country's first ever bone marrow transplant centre for Iraqis suffering from leukaemia.

Crucially, after much prayer, I came to the very difficult and painful conclusion that Saddam had to be removed from power, and it caused a stir when I said so publicly. Here was the director of a major international centre for peace saying that a war was necessary for the sake of the Iraqi people. Fortunately, everybody at the ICR supported me in this view. Metaphorically, they had been in Iraq with me over the years and, indeed, my bishop had been there with me literally.

Sadly, though I repeatedly urged the British and American governments to engage with the country's religious and tribal leaders after the war, it was a long time before anyone did so – by which time, Saddam's reign of terror had been replaced by bloody religious sectarianism which has since cost tens, if not hundreds, of thousands of lives. Eventually, in 2007, the new commander of the Coalition forces in Iraq, General David Petraeus, asked me to work on this issue and, with funding from the Pentagon, I brought together the group that we now call the "High Council of Religious Leaders in Iraq". For two years, while this handful of eminent Muslims met together, the level of violence fell dramatically. Then the Bush administration left office at the beginning of 2009, our funding stopped, and the fire is again flaring up.

Even as I have been writing this book, the heat has seriously intensified. This time, it is because the pastor of a small church in Florida announced his intention of burning several hundred copies of the Qur'an. The effect in Baghdad has been tremendous. First, a colonel came to tell me that there were threats to blow up both me and St George's Church. Our security was seriously increased, but the next day something awful happened: four of the soldiers guarding our compound were shot dead by drive-by gunmen. The remaining soldiers went to bury them, so we were left with very little protection. All the Christians in Baghdad were terrified. I managed to get word to my friend Grand Ayatollah Hussein al-Sadr and he contacted Grand Ayatollah Ali al-Sistani – the most authoritative figure in Iraq; and within a few hours the latter had issued a *fatwa* saying that there must be no action against the Christians or their churches. The following weekend my congregation was much depleted as people were too frightened to come to church, but there were still several hundred of us and we worshipped fearlessly!

The "Burn a Qur'an Day" in Florida was eventually called off, but we have had our own bonfires here. The first Sunday after this terrible event was Holy Cross Day, when the tradition is that after the service a fire is lit outside the church in front of a cross, and as people leave they jump over the fire to kiss the cross. This year it seemed so powerfully symbolic. On the other side of the world there was talk of a fire that would have brought nothing but destruction, but here the fire that burned was a celebration of life, light and love.

This is just one small example of the dangers that are part and parcel of living out one's faith under fire. I never considered such dangers before following God's call, but the fact is, I know well that He is with me through whatever trials and troubles I face. The truth is, He enables me to live without fear. People often ask me why I am not scared and I always give the same answer: perfect love casts out all fear.

By 2005 I had left Coventry Cathedral to work permanently in Iraq as vicar of St George's Church in Baghdad, based just outside the Green Zone. Shortly I will explain how God intervened in my life to bring about this transition. But before I do, I must pause to reflect on the ways in which God prepared and equipped me for this work. It is always humbling to look back and see how God uses every experience, good or bad, to move us forward in His purposes for our lives.

I am not the same colour as my brother and sister. They were born perfectly white and I was not. We had the same parents, but in me the Anglo-Indian heritage of my father came through, so that my skin is dark and my hair black. I could easily pass for an Iraqi. This may seem a small point, but it is very significant. If it were not for my appearance, I would be at even greater risk than I am, because I might be mistaken for an American.

By the time I was ten, I had decided that I wanted both to go into medicine and to be a priest. My primary school teacher told me I couldn't do both, but today I have not only the biggest church in Iraq but also one of the best medical and dental clinics in the whole of Baghdad. When the clinic is not open, people often come to me for help instead. Only God knew why I needed to be trained for both the operating theatre and the pulpit.

I became an Anglican when I was a boy. My parents were Strict and Particular Baptists who were also Pentecostals, and the Church of England was frowned upon in our home. But I was more influenced by an old lady who lived opposite us, who was a High Anglican, and I started going to her church. Fortunately, my parents didn't stop me – they just regarded it as youthful rebellion! However, it was the perfect schooling for leading a congregation of people from Orthodox and Catholic backgrounds in Iraq, where the only Western-led church is Anglican.

My father instilled in me a fascination for Judaism and a love for the Jews, and my studies at theological college only deepened and broadened my interest in the Middle East and its three dominant religions: first Judaism, then Eastern Christianity and finally Islam. The crisis over Jews for Jesus at Cambridge then drew me into interfaith relations.

Finally, I developed multiple sclerosis. It is difficult to see this as something positive, but the truth is that if I had not fallen ill with MS, I would probably have continued climbing the ladder of the church hierarchy and applied for more senior appointments.

So I am aware that God trains and prepares us through all of life's experiences. Sometimes He sees fit to impose on us things that we do not view as "the best" for our lives, but He sees the greater purpose and allows such things so that we will do what He wants us to do or go where He wants us to go. In all of this, I profoundly believe that God can and will use such adverse circumstances for His glory. The words of the apostle Paul are true for me, as they are for you: "And we know that in all things God works for the good of those who love him, who have been called according to his purpose" (Romans 8:28).

3

THE NATURE OF FAITH

At St George's we begin every service with the following words: *"Allah hu ma'na wa Ruh al-Qudus ma'na aithan."* They mean, "God is here, and His Holy Spirit is here." This simple phrase sums up my understanding of faith under fire – that we need not live in fear because God is present with us at all times.

When we turn to Jesus and make Him the Lord of our lives, we are allowing the kingdom of God to come in all its fullness. What do I mean by that? I mean that to be a real person of faith we cannot view or attempt things from a human point of view. We have to see things as God sees them and allow Him to work through us to accomplish that which in human terms is impossible! This is the essence of supernatural living – hearing God and living in obedience to Him, even when it doesn't make logical sense. When our understanding of our relationship with God undergoes this "shift", it transports us into a different realm of living. We no longer view events in a "normal" way, but in a heavenly way. We begin to truly understand the prayer, "Thy will be done on earth as it is in heaven." In this statement Jesus was teaching us to move in faith and shift our vision from the natural to the supernatural. As we do that we will begin to be exposed to the miraculous. But this will never happen until we begin to open our eyes to God's supernatural power.

Being thrust into the fire accelerates this process. So often in our situation here in Baghdad, we have no other option but to live by faith, in total dependence on a supernatural God who constantly intervenes on our behalf. People ask me, "Do you really see God moving supernaturally in Iraq?" The fact is, I do. I have never seen so much of the miraculous power of God anywhere on my travels as I have in Iraq – from people being healed to babies being raised from the dead to God providing for us when we have nothing. When people offer to pray for us in Iraq I often respond by saying, "Thank you, I know that God will answer your prayers."

Here it is often the children who pray most effectively. Recently, Ian, a friend of mine who is a priest in the USA, was seriously ill in hospital on a ventilator. The children of St George's prayed for him daily and he made a miraculously speedy recovery. When news reached us that Ian had been discharged from hospital, the children made me arrange a party, so that they could thank God for answering their prayers.

When I think of faith and what it means to live that faith out under difficult circumstances, I am constantly drawn to the words of the Nicene Creed – the statement of our fundamental beliefs as Christians. I want to go through each section and tell you what it means to me here in Iraq.

Faith

We believe in one God,
the Father, the Almighty,
maker of heaven and earth,
of all that is,
seen and unseen.

For me, surrounded by a majority Muslim community, the belief in one God is essential. At times Christians are accused of believing in three gods, so we are continually explaining that despite understanding that God is Trinity, to us He is also one God. We may not entirely understand the doctrine of the Trinity, but then there are many things in our faith that we cannot understand completely. There is much mystery involved in the miracle of our faith!

Also essential to us is the fact that God is the Creator of everything. In Iraq, we believe that this land is the home of creation and the very site of the Garden of Eden. My fundamental belief is that God is the Creator of heaven and earth, of all that is seen and unseen. Once again there is mystery involved and we cannot understand everything, but we know that one day when we see Him, we will.

We believe in one Lord, Jesus Christ,
the only Son of God,
eternally begotten of the Father,
God from God, Light from Light,
true God from true God,
begotten, not made,
of one Being with the Father;
through him all things were made.

The truth of the Incarnation is central to everything I believe, everything I know as I live out my faith under fire. It is vital to live in the truth that God is not distant from us, because He has come and lived among us – and not just among us, but as one of us. In Jesus, our God has become our brother. Christ also suffered, so in Him we have a God with an intimate knowledge of human suffering. He is not impassive or disconnected from our own suffering. In Jesus we have a God who has been in the line of fire.

God is a God of relationship and it is His desire to be in constant communion with us. Throughout my day I feel God's presence and talk to Him continually. I regularly teach others how to hear God's voice, and almost weekly in our services at St George's people will come forward and report what the Lord has said to them.

> *For us and for our salvation*
> *he came down from heaven:*
> *was incarnate of the Holy Spirit*
> *and the Virgin Mary*
> *and was made man.*

That God came to dwell among us is essential, but so is the reason why He came: to bring us salvation and to enable us to be one with Him. It is so important to us here in Iraq that, by the power of the Holy Spirit, He entered this world through a young woman called Mariam (Mary) – a woman who is so much a part of our lives here. Yet she was as ordinary and insignificant as we are. Like many here who have suffered the tragedy of war, she too saw her beloved son suffer and die. Mary endured what many mothers here have endured. Again, she is not a distant figure – here she is greatly respected as the mother of our Lord, who shows us by her example how to welcome the Almighty, how to accept pain and how, in Him, to overcome.

> *For our sake he was crucified under Pontius Pilate;*
> *he suffered death and was buried.*
> *On the third day he rose again*
> *in accordance with the Scriptures;*
> *he ascended into heaven*
> *and is seated at the right hand of the Father.*
> *He will come again in glory to judge the living and*
> *the dead,*
> *and his kingdom will have no end.*

The very heart of our creed speaks about the suffering and ultimate sacrifice of our God. Jesus, our Saviour, was crucified on the cross. As a symbol, the cross is very meaningful to us in Baghdad – though it is not a comfortable image, but a reminder of a cruel death. In the midst of our suffering here, our faith is symbolized by an instrument of torture and execution (which is something we too often forget). If our emblem were an axe or a gun or an electric chair, we might be more acutely aware of the cost and nature of our faith. But in this city where so many Christians have been killed, where I myself have experienced so much opposition and aggression, my faith seems more real than ever when I grasp that my Lord also lived "under fire" and ultimately was killed. Yet death could not hold Him; He broke its power, and this means that I know death cannot hold me either, and I genuinely do not need to fear it. As my congregation often remind me when any of our people are killed: one day we are going to see and be with our God.

Of equal significance is the fact of the ascension of God incarnate. This is a truth I have thought about a lot, ever since I became the vicar of a church that bore the name of this event. There are many aspects of this that mean a lot to me, but most significant is the fact that Jesus, as a human being, was taken into heaven. Representing us, with scars on His hands, His feet and His side, Jesus took into the heavenly realm all the brokenness and suffering of humanity, demonstrating that one day, through Him, we too will be accepted and welcomed home. As the old Andraé Crouch song says, "Soon and very soon, we are going to see the King" – and there will be no more suffering, crying or dying!

What is more, we know that Jesus is going to return. He will come to judge humankind and to take those who love Him to be with Him forever. Every day in Baghdad, I am surrounded by people who do not love God and who commit acts of violence in His name. Every day, I remember that God will be their Judge. Every day, too, I recall that in Jesus' tomb the cloth that had been wrapped round His head was found folded after His resurrection. This is a powerful oriental symbol, taken from the dining table. If you folded your napkin when you left the table, it indicated to your servants that you hadn't finished and were coming back. The cloth from around the head of Jesus was folded because He is coming back! And if He is coming back I know I have nothing to fear, because I can be confident that one day I will be with Him in person.

We believe in the Holy Spirit,
the Lord, the giver of Life,
who proceeds from the Father and the Son.
With the Father and the Son he is worshipped
and glorified.
He has spoken through the prophets.
We believe in one holy catholic and apostolic Church.
We acknowledge one baptism for the forgiveness
of sins.
We look for the resurrection of the dead,
and the life of the world to come. Amen.

As I reflect on my faith under fire, I see that it is the Holy Spirit who inspires me, enables me and makes God so real to me. He "who proceeds from the Father and the Son" conveys my worship back to them. He enables me to work in a supernatural way. He is not limited by the laws of time and space that govern us. In Baghdad, we see the glory and the power of God constantly; we see His signs and wonders and His angels all the time. (I will write more about these things later in this book.)

When I consider the closing lines of the creed, a remark by Lord Hylton, the chair of my Foundation Advisory Board, comes to mind. After his first visit to St George's, he wrote, "I have been to the church of the future." What is "the church of the future"? It is a church that is one, holy, catholic – that is, universal – and apostolic. In St George's we are Catholic, Orthodox and Protestant, but we are one because we all love and follow one Jesus. We have all been baptized into one faith; we know that we have one creed and one future, one resurrection and one belief. I know that my faith and hope are based on the love of God, with whom I will one day live forever. I will be reunited with all those who have gone before me into the heavenly realms. This is the faith that, with hope and love, sustains me.

Hope

Hope is one of the key components of our faith. Hope may be "futuristic" in that it always looks forward, but it enables us continually to keep our eyes fixed on Jesus, even in the midst of our greatest difficulties. Biblical hope is not something vague or intangible, but is solid and dependable. You have to have real hope when someone is holding a gun against your head. When I think back to my days as a vicar in England, the problems people used to bring to me seem fairly trivial compared with the trials we face each day in Baghdad. But whether our problems are great or small, the need for hope is very real for us all. In hope we have to prise our eyes away from our problems, whatever they are, and look intently to Jesus. We have hope because we are loved by Him and He is our future.

It is profoundly important that the Hebrew name of God means "the One who was and is and is to come". (I cannot actually write this name as a result of my studies at the yeshiva as a young man. In the Jewish religion, the name of God could be spoken only by the high priest, once a year in the Holy of Holies in the temple, on the sacred Day of Atonement, Yom Kippur. I don't even write the English word "God" in full in the regular updates I send to my supporters, because many of them are Orthodox Jews. Instead, as they would, I simply write "G-d".) Our God, then, is One who is past, present and future. This means that if God is constantly present with us, we always have hope. His presence has the ability to transform any situation. How we need to embrace hope and believe in transformation! To do that we do not look at everything through natural eyes, but spiritual eyes. At this very moment I can look out of my window and see bombed buildings, razor wire, concrete barricades and tanks. This scene presents me with a choice: either I can think, "What a terrible place this is" or I can think, "Isn't it wonderful that God has chosen to presence Himself here of all places!" Things may look very grim, but with the Almighty everything can change.

In a few hours' time, over a thousand of my congregation will be here to worship. All of them have experienced hardship and many of them have seen terrible things. They may have had their homes destroyed, or their husbands or children kidnapped or killed, or been injured in an explosion themselves. And yet they all have hope. I remember one day when I was crying after some of our people had been killed and the continued loss of life was so great that it completely overwhelmed me. Some of our children came to me and said, "Don't cry, Daddy," – this is what all the children call me – "they are with Jesus now and He speaks the same language as them – Aramaic."

Even as I was writing just now, Nabila, the woman who looks after me at St George's, came in to see me. I have been telling the congregation that at Lent we don't just need to give things up, but we need also to take up listening to God. Nabila told me that she had been listening to God and had just heard Him speaking to her. She has been so worried about her daughter, who has gone missing. Every day she hopes she will come back but she doesn't. Today, though, God has told her that her hope is in Him. She knows she must take up her cross every day and follow Jesus – but now she knows that it is not just a cross of pain, but also a cross of hope. Indeed, the cross is our only hope, both now and for the future.

The cross is a paradox – a terrible symbol of agony and pain, and yet representative of our hope for the future. We can spend so much time focusing on the suffering it represents that we forget that it speaks of a glorious future. Likewise, we can spend so long contemplating the difficulties of our present situation that we forget what God has in store for us. In this regard there is one quotation that has helped me more than any other. In *The Pilgrim's Progress*, John Bunyan relates that when Pilgrim comes to the Palace Beautiful he is asked: "By what means do you find your annoyances, at times, as if they were vanquished?" He replies: "When I think what I saw at the cross, that will do it; and when I look upon my broidered coat, that will do it; also when I look into the roll that I carry in my bosom, that will do it; and when my thoughts wax warm about whither I am going, that will do it."

In simple words, "When I see all that God has provided for me, that keeps me going." When I look at the Bible, God's Holy Word, that sustains me. When I think of what Jesus did for me on the cross, that causes me to persevere. When I think about heaven, my ultimate destination, that energizes me. People often ask me how I keep going in Baghdad, and this is how: I think of Pilgrim's words and find that they are true for me too. I keep going because I have a hope which is all-embracing, all-consuming, unending and eternal. As long as we who believe in Jesus hold on to hope, we can do anything. There is no such word as "no" in the Christian's vocabulary! If we are really following Christ, we hold on to hope and will always achieve that which God has given us to do.

Love

I've said many times that whenever we commit ourselves to doing what God wants us to do, He gives us a love for doing it. That is why I love being where I am and I love what I'm doing. Love, along with faith and hope, is the third quality that sustains me.

At the end of every service at St George's we say together, "*Al-Hubb, al-Hubb, al-Hubb*" – which means, "We must love, love, love." "Love" sums up all we are trying to do in Iraq. I entirely agree with the apostle Paul when he says in 1 Corinthians 13:13 that love is the greatest of the three great virtues. Love was the key feature of the life and teaching of our Lord and it is foundational to all our endeavours in Iraq. I long for the day when everyone sees and accepts its virtue – and not just Christians, but those of other traditions as well.

Love is vital, but love is not easy – certainly not the love that Jesus spoke about, since He told us to love our enemies. This is one aspect of His teaching we often find difficult to practise because, generally speaking, we do not love our enemies very much. Some Christians will say, "I have to love you, but I don't have to like you." But I have a big problem with this sentiment, because I believe it cheapens the love of God. Personally, I have never liked anybody I have not loved, and I have never loved anybody I haven't liked! The love of God will always highlight some quality we can value in every person, because every person is valued by Him. Therefore, I take the command to love very seriously. Whenever I encounter a person who is difficult to love, I pray, "Lord, help me to love them!" In my experience this never requires a miracle, just a change of attitude and an act of will.

Often, people who seem "unlovable" begin to change when they are loved. I have seen this happen many times in Palestine and Iraq. The most radical example of this was Sheikh Talal Sidr. He was one of the founders and former leaders of the Islamic resistance movement Hamas, which is committed to the destruction of the State of Israel. When I started working with him – and loving him – even Christians told me that I should not be doing so. But he became the biggest proponent of peace I have ever met. He left Hamas and when anyone asked him what he was doing now, he would say, "I am pulling up thorns and planting flowers." When I asked him why he had changed so much, he told me it was because we had loved him. When he died in 2006, even Israeli members of the Knesset went to his funeral in out-of-bounds Hebron.

In Iraq, too, we have seen people change when they were shown real love. I have often said that one of the principal causes of terrorism is the issue of loss. People resort to violence when they feel something has been taken away from them. Giving love to them, instead of returning violence with violence, is returning to them something that has been lost. Giving love can radically change even seemingly hopeless situations. This is why Jesus tells us to love those who do not love us. Much of my work in religious sectarianism is simply about showing love to the unlovely.

I have often said that St George's is the best church I have ever been a part of, and it is the best for one reason: its love. I have never before been loved as I've been loved by these people – and I have never loved a group of people as I love the people of St George's. All of them, from the very youngest to the oldest, express a sincere love. For that reason I don't like being away from the church frequently. I leave periodically only to raise the huge sums of money we need to provide food and medical care for the people here. Whenever I ask a member of the congregation why they come to St George's, without fail they will say it is because of the love the people have for one another here. When you are surrounded by so many atrocities caused by hatred, love becomes all the more important. And our love must be holistic – we first love God and then we love each other.

Love is not the reason I stepped into the fire, but it is love that keeps me here. I recall that back in the chapel of my theological college in Cambridge, the following words hung on the wall: "He who has called you will not fail you." I am constantly aware that the love of God will never fail me. God will never fail me. I have no fear of living in the fire, but rather an immense joy because I know God's love and the love of the people around me. Perfect love casts out all fear. What I have is God's perfect love.

And now these three remain: faith, hope and love.
But the greatest of these is love.

1 Corinthians 13:13

4

Faith Amidst Tragedy

few years ago I was one of the speakers at the annual Home Focus Conference of Holy Trinity, Brompton, and found myself listening to an evangelist called Simon Guillebaud speaking about his experiences in Burundi. Simon was working there (at the time reputedly the most dangerous war zone on earth) right after the atrocities that had engulfed the country and its neighbour, Rwanda, in 1994. Nowadays I don't get many opportunities to sit in a conference and listen to other speakers, but this young man said something I will never forget. Caroline was with me and she wrote down the words in her Bible: "I only knew that Jesus was all I needed when He was all I had left." Simon had discovered that this powerful truth was true for him in Burundi and it is certainly true for me in Baghdad.

As I look around my church, I see so many people who have lost so much. Their loved ones are dead, in many cases killed in the most terrible ways. As I travel to other places in the world it is hard to express the horror of the situation here in ways that people can understand – and I have to try to remember that. Recently I went to the USA to attend a friend's wedding in Lexington, Kentucky. I arrived there only days after some children in Baghdad had been cruelly murdered. That evening I was asked to preach at my friend's church and I made the mistake of mentioning this incident and relating the way in which these innocent children died. Two people in the congregation rushed out of the church and were physically sick. That night I vowed I would never repeat the story and to this day I have not mentioned it again. The violence involved was indeed the worst I have ever seen.

I have seen so much brokenness and tragedy in Iraq – on a scale beyond anything I have witnessed anywhere else – that I simply cannot write about it. It is just too awful. In the face of such loss, all I and those who have suffered so much can do is return to Simon's profound words. This is the one thing that everyone at St George's can agree on: even if they have lost everything, they still have Jesus. In this regard I am reminded of what Augustine of Hippo once said about Christians: we are an Easter people and "Alleluia" is our song.

We are indeed an Easter people. Like all Easter people, our symbol is the cross – a symbol of immense pain and suffering, a symbol of death, but also a symbol of hope, of life and of resurrection. That which represents a cruel, violent death also represents new and eternal life. I myself always wear around my neck a cross made from nails from the ruins of the old Coventry cathedral – itself a symbol of resurrection and reconciliation. A similar cross of nails stands on our altar in St George's and most of our congregation wear smaller versions specially made by the church. Easter is central to what we believe and "Alleluia" is indeed our song – it is what we sing as we process into church each week.

Not long ago St George's was seriously damaged in a bomb blast and our clinic, including our pharmacy and laboratory, was all but destroyed. A PowerPoint presentation was made by the Iraqis to show to our synod, with pictures of the complex before and after the bombing, and finally after all our buildings had been restored. No words were spoken during the presentation; the images were accompanied simply by our choir singing "Alleluia".

Pain and joy in the fire

We may have suffered tragedy and loss, but we still have Jesus. Faith does not take away our suffering, but it certainly enables us to cope with tragedy. Life is difficult, but we know that God does not leave us on our own. In our suffering we are constantly aware of the suffering and glory of the cross. Often, in the space of one day in Iraq, we experience both "Good Friday moments" and "Easter Sunday moments" – the devastation of death and loss being followed by the glory of resurrection, darkness being obliterated by light. For those of us "in the fire", tragedy only makes our faith more real.

So, for me, to serve in the fire involves immense pain mixed with joy. But we must never forget those who actually have no choice but to live in the fire – the thousands in our church community, the millions in Iraq. We must never forget their hardships. I have no regrets that I am called to serve in the fire. I wish that my people did not have to live in such circumstances, but I feel nothing but joy that I am serving with them. We are in love with each other and the Almighty.

At the same time, our people also have huge needs, which

have to be met: for medical help, for food, for accommodation. The first is met by the large and successful clinic we have installed in the church complex, which provides medical and dental treatment for a hundred or more people a day. All of this care is offered free of charge to the whole of the local community, not just to the congregation. If anyone needs to go to hospital, even to have surgery, we have very strong links with Baghdad's private Christian hospital and can pay for their treatment there.

As regards food, we provide everyone in the congregation with groceries each week after church. Accommodation is more difficult. We have very limited safe accommodation, but we regularly help a large number of people to pay their rent. Each month, I have to raise $175,000 for this purpose. It is not easy, but with God's help I usually manage it. In the midst of tragedy people need to be helped. People outside Iraq are always asking me how they can support us, and my invariable answer is simply: prayer and money. These are practical ways to show love. Constantly, people say to me: "We need to help the Iraqis to become self-sufficient. We can't keep supporting them forever." But the fact is, these people are living in the fire. If we could put the flames out, we would. We are forever trying, but the fire continues to rage. This very week, several of my people have been killed. This hurts so much, and yet I know the Lord is always with us.

One day, I was contacted by a pastor from New Jersey, who told me of a ten-year-old girl in his congregation called Joanna. She had been saving up for a dog when she heard me preach at her church, and had just been to see him and had given him all the money she had saved – $80 – and said she wanted it to go to the children of St George's Church in Baghdad. How touched I was by this story! It is people like Joanna who sustain me amidst all the tragedy here. It is people like her who give us hope and enable us to keep going. In the following week, I told this story of little Joanna many times, and in response people gave over $20,000 for St George's – and also $500 for Joanna's dog!

It is glimpses of hope such as these, and my total trust and dependence upon the Almighty, that get me through the hardship. Seeing love visibly demonstrated is hugely encouraging. My friend Rodney Howard-Browne, speaking about the lack of passion in preachers' lives, commented that they needed to "see the love of God". He then said directly to me, "Andrew, you have seen the love of God in the eyes of the children." He was so right. I am surrounded by people who have nothing, but although this is part of the tragedy of Iraq, it is also, strangely, a means by which God demonstrates His glory, because He always answers our prayers and provides for us. The pain of those who do not have what they need – not only money but medicine, food, accommodation – is very real. I watch American TV in my room in Baghdad and it makes me very angry when I hear (as I often do) that "If you give, you will get." My people have nothing to give – or nothing to give except love. I do believe that God gives when we give – I see this all the time – but what He promises is to meet our needs, "according to his glorious riches in Christ Jesus" (Philippians 4:19). This has been my experience. As I give to our people in the midst of tragedy, I know that what I am giving comes from God. And those who receive it also acknowledge that God is the giver, the One who meets all their needs.

I realize that my experience in the fire is totally different to what most people experience, but at the same time I know I would not be able to minister well in the safety of British or American suburbia – though, of course, the people there still need to be loved and many have serious needs. I know that I am called to serve the needs of those in tragedy, which are both practical and spiritual. One other thing that all of our people need, without exception, is love. It is love that holds us together – love for God and love for each other. We often say that our love has to be as radical and as extreme as the hatred that surrounds us. Of course, whenever we talk about love we are talking about the possibility of pain. In any human relationship, where there is love, there can always be hurt. The object of our love can always change, can always leave us – or we ourselves can change or leave. If nothing else, death will divide us in the end. God, however, is a different matter. He does not change, He does not leave us. He is always love and He is always present. Every day, I experience that love. How do I know for sure that God loves me? Because I feel it. Because the Bible tells me so. Because I am in constant communication with God, and constantly He answers my prayers.

A people of hope

Despite the fact that St George's is constantly under fire, it is the happiest church I have ever served in. We may be beset by huge problems, but we also have huge joy because the Lord does meet all our needs and our faith gives us hope in tragedy.

Our hope is very real and together we are a people of hope. Constantly at St George's we talk about the role of "the land between the rivers", or Mesopotamia, as it was originally called in the Bible. This land, modern-day Iraq, is mentioned all the time in Scripture – only Israel/Palestine is mentioned more often. Special to all of us are the closing verses of Isaiah 19, which talk about a highway being built from Egypt to Assyria (that is, Iraq) through Israel and describe Assyria as God's "handiwork". This gives us all so much hope. We do not live in fear, because we know that from the beginning (the Garden of Eden was in Mesopotamia) to the end foreseen by Isaiah, the Lord is with us. Often we say that if the world began here, maybe it will also end here.

It may sound very strange to say that in the midst of such great tragedy we are joyful and hopeful and have no fear, but it is true. Everyone who could afford to flee Iraq has now gone. First, it was to Jordan or to Sweden, but when they closed their doors to Iraqis, people fled instead to Syria or, latterly, Lebanon. Those who are still left in Iraq are those who have nowhere to go. They are the ones who couldn't get out, because they are seriously poor. Yet, at the same time, it is true to say that those in our church who remain are here because they do not want to leave. I often say to our people: we who are left must stay. We must stay because we know that God is involved in Iraq and we are part of His story. We know without doubt that the words we say at the start of each service are absolutely true: "*Allah hu ma'na wa Ruh al-Qudus ma'na aithan.*" ("God is here, and His Holy Spirit is here.")

Many people look at Iraq, as well as many other examples of human suffering, and ask, "How can a God of love allow such evil?" It is a very difficult question – one about which many books have been written with conflicting views. Theologians grappling with this issue have viewed God either as One who is not completely omniscient and omnipotent, or else as One who is well aware of evil but chooses to allow it. God is pictured as someone who can't intervene or who chooses to do nothing. At the heart of Christian theology, however, is the concept of a partially inaugurated eschatology, and it is here that I find a level of understanding. In other words, the kingdom of God is here and now, and yet not fully administered. The things of heaven can and do happen on earth, but so can things influenced by the present evil age. From the time of the resurrection of Christ to His second coming, God's kingdom exists alongside the kingdom of darkness. Thus the devil has real influence and power now, but this will be brought to an end when Christ returns in power.

This is the theology I hold to and is what I think Jesus Himself believed. Was this not what He was referring to when He instructed us to pray, "Your will be done on earth as it is in heaven"? Thus I and many of the leadership team at St George's see the trauma all around us as the consequence of this partially inaugurated eschatology, as this evil age continues to make its presence known despite the coming of God's kingdom. I have never had to consider these matters so deeply in any other parish I have served in. But here in Baghdad I have often sat down and discussed it with my team, because here the issue is so real.

Any tragedy – such as the tragedy of 9/11 – tends to make it so. People ask, "How can God allow such things to happen?" Yet, I have to point out: I have never once heard this

The bright globe in the sky is not the moon, but one of the many strange things we see all the time. Are they wheels like Ezekiel saw? All we know is that they are a sign of the presence of God.

Some of the young girls at the church surrounded by the orbs of glory.

The young children at the church preparing for their first communion. They know that they are called to follow the way of the Lord, come what may.

Children have also been destroyed by the violence...

...but are an important part of the life of the church.

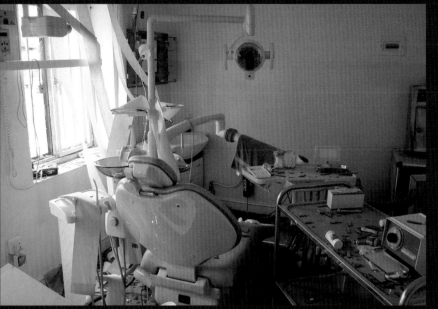

The dental surgery in the church is wrecked by a bomb.

The army comes to visit the dentist!

The love we have for one another sustains us all. With young Fulla and Mariam.

With my normal security team of Iraqi soldiers!

The aftermath of
a major bombing
outside the church
that destroyed
much of our
building and killed
144 people.

Majid, our lay pastor, at the baptism of his daughter shortly before he was kidnapped.

Adults and children are baptised into the faith under fire.

The funeral procession after the killing of 58 people in the Church of our Lady of Deliverance on 31 October 2010. It is surrounded by the cloud of glory that we have become so accustomed to.

The day I was presented the 2010 Civil Courage Prize in New York. With me is Maen, a young Iraqi Christian who I rescued as a child six years ago. This was the first time I had seen him and here he is with his mother May.

After church people stand in line to receive their food for the week.

This man's father and brother have been killed because they loved Jesus.

Despite the danger, Faiz is ordained as the first ever Iraqi Anglican Minister.

Talking to the troops in Baghdad.

A girl giving flowers to Major General Andrew Farquhol when the army came to look round the church compound.

The children and the choir marching round the church compound at Easter 2009.

At an event of the Knights Templar.

question asked by ordinary members of my congregation at St George's. Why not? Once again, I come back to the matter of love. It is God's unending love that gives us hope and purpose. It is His love that sustains us and holds us together. My people see the suffering of Christ in our tragedy and yet they find, as Thomas Aquinas put it, that it was "the love of Christ and not His suffering that was redemptive".

Thus, in the midst of tragedy, when we have lost everything and Jesus is all we have left, we know that He is all we need.

5

FAITH UNDER ATTACK

I have been under attack many times in my life, though it is not always clear whether this has been because of who I am and what I am doing or simply because of my faith. To my mind, the two things are inseparable. I do what I do because I am sure that my Lord has called me to do it. Much of this work, however, is seen as a direct threat to those whose intent is to cause violence and they will attack anyone who obstructs what they are trying to achieve.

Looking back, I can see that some of the attacks on me have been opportunistic and may have been made simply because I am a Westerner. Others have clearly been targeted at me very deliberately. I will never forget the day when I was temporarily kidnapped and thrown into a room that had severed human fingers and toes strewn over the floor. I thought, as my captors wanted me to, that my digits would be next. My response in such a situation was not well thought out – I just wanted God to preserve me and get me out of there, and thankfully He did. On another occasion, pictures of me were plastered on walls around Baghdad bearing a simple message: "Wanted, dead or alive". The British embassy made me leave the country for a while, though happily it was not long before I was able to return to the people and the land I love.

It used to amaze me that a minister like me should have to go to church each week wearing body armour and in an armoured vehicle surrounded by Iraqi military. There can't be many ministers in the world who set out to conduct their services like this. Nowadays things are a bit different and I live on the church compound itself, surrounded by bomb-proof barricades, but the number of police and soldiers detailed to guard us by the Iraqi government is still phenomenal. Recently, when I went to Kurdistan with Lord Hylton, more than 120 soldiers were sent to escort us out of Baghdad. Once we were safely outside the capital, our bodyguard was reduced to the usual thirty-five. The children of St George's tell me that the soldiers are also like my "children", so I have referred to them as such ever since.

The situation in Iraq is different in many ways from my time in Israel and Palestine. There my relationships were much more political, so any attacks tended to be politically motivated. Here I am with my people, God's people, who are under fire for their faith, and the attacks, I'm sure, originate from a spiritual source. As well as St George's, I have a congregation at the American Embassy chapel, which includes many military personnel who have also come under attack, and some have been wounded or even killed. Of course, they are not fighting for their faith, but many of their adversaries regard them as soldiers of an evil force from the Christian West and see the conflict with them in spiritual terms. There is very little one can do to persuade people otherwise.

Whilst I am aware that I am constantly at risk and must

listen to those in charge of my security, I am acutely aware that the members of my congregation have no such security. They may not have my high profile, but they are all at risk because they are known to be followers of Jesus of Nazareth.

Even as I was writing that last sentence on Easter Sunday, I heard the sound of a huge explosion. It sounded like a rocket landing about half a mile away. I just continued writing. Two minutes later there was another, much larger, explosion and our building shuddered and some windows shattered. My security men ran in to make sure that I hadn't been injured by flying glass, and then the British ambassador rang, no doubt to check that I was still alive. There was a commotion for a while and the children who live in the compound were all crying as we set out to survey the damage. Indeed, the damage was bad (though nowhere near as bad as that caused by another bomb that landed on us five months earlier).We learned that it was a car bomb, targeting the Iranian Embassy. Over forty people had been killed. My adopted son, David, visited the scene and actually went out picking up pieces of human bodies. Some birds even fell, dead, from the sky.

I wondered whether people would still turn up for our service. But this was our Resurrection Day and, regardless of this tragedy, people flocked to the service. We had invited the Governor of Baghdad and, despite the fact that his office lay between us and the Iranian Embassy and had also suffered in the blast, he still came. He presented us with a large arrangement of flowers and assured the congregation that he was not about to abandon us.

After the service, as everyone filed out, they were given "friendship" bracelets made by the children at River Church in New Jersey, as well as their groceries for the week. I had said goodbye to hundreds of people, but some stayed behind as the choir continued to sing. Suddenly, as I later wrote in my spiritual update, "heaven opened… the worship was the most amazing I had ever experienced in Iraq – there was such joy as we sang of the Lord's resurrection and glory. He was indeed with us."

The targeting of the Iranian Embassy shows that it is not just the Christians who are under attack in Iraq. There is literally not one community or group here that is spared. Everyone has enemies and is suffering persecution. The fact that the suffering is universal does not make it any easier to bear, but nevertheless, unlike most people here, I choose to be here. I believe I have been sent here by God and for that reason I have no desire to leave. I accept that I will be constantly under attack. We may not all experience bombings, but all of us will experience spiritual opposition and attack whilst we are determined to walk in God's will.

That said, the threat to Christians in Iraq has been very severe. Last year alone, ninety-three members of my congregation were killed. The threat is particularly great for those who convert to Christianity. I baptized thirteen adults secretly last year. Eleven of them were dead within a week. I always warn those who want to be baptized as converts how dangerous it is, but they say they still want to follow Jesus. As I stand at the front of the church each week, I see the families of those who have been killed or kidnapped and am quickly reminded of those who are no longer with us. I have often tried to think of ways to protect my people, but I cannot. When they are with me, to some extent they have the benefit of my bodyguard, but there is no way to provide complete protection. Bombs can always hit us from below and rockets from above.

As the violence in Iraq increased in recent years, many of Iraq's Christians fled abroad, and those in Baghdad who could not afford to do so took refuge instead in the northern province where their families all originated. To this day, some 2,700 years after Jonah arrived there "in the belly of a great fish", the people are still keeping the faith. Mosul, the provincial capital of Nineva, which faces the ruins of the ancient city of Nineveh across the Tigris, is still full of Assyrians, but now most of them are Christians. Seven centuries after Jonah's visit, "doubting" Thomas passed through on his way to India and when he saw that the people in Nineveh worshipped the God of Abraham, Isaac and Jacob, he told them their Messiah had come. Thus, the majority of people in Nineva today are Christians – but that does not mean they are safe. It was not long before al-Qa'ida's men also made the journey to Mosul and began targeting Christians there, kidnapping, torturing and killing them. What had briefly seemed like a haven has become a place of great danger, and many Christians are now fleeing back to Baghdad.

Christianity in Iraq is under very vicious attack. It is not a question of debate – there is no debate here. It is a question of abduction, torture, rape and murder. Christians are forced to pay *jizya*, the tax historically imposed by Islamic states on non-Muslims, in effect as "protection money". So, things are very difficult. We never know which of our people will be targeted next. What is most disturbing is that much of the violence is committed in God's name. I am constantly reminded of the words of Archbishop William Temple: "When religion goes wrong, it goes very wrong."

The suffering church

I am regularly asked about my thoughts on the suffering church and persecution. I respond by speaking about three Ps that lie at the heart of persecution: *perception*, *proclamation* and *practice*.

Perception

The first reason for persecution is people's perception of each other. Recently, I was sitting with some Muslim and Christian friends in Baghdad and the subject of recognizing adherents to one another's faith came up. Each of them was certain that they could immediately recognize those who were Muslims and those who were Christians. In fact, they went into great detail about how the "other" looked. To be honest, I cannot tell the difference between most Iraqi Christians and Muslims, yet my friends were adamant that they could and their perceptions were very real to them. These perceptions are also, of course, shared by those radicals who are intent on persecution.

Proclamation

Then there is the issue of proclamation. All the Christians I know, in many different countries, feel that their faith is something they must not keep to themselves, and in Iraq it is no different. Christians here are careful not to be overtly evangelistic, for that would be reckless, but they certainly proclaim their faith and most will wear a cross very visibly around their necks. When I talk to Christians who have been kidnapped, they always report that they were pressurized to say the Islamic words of conversion. Most of them refused – to them, their faith is the most important thing in their life. A few have told me that they did say the words, because they were afraid that otherwise they would be killed; but when they were released, they came to me and confessed what they had done. I have always told them they are forgiven – God will not hold it against them – and invariably they have been even more strict in their faith ever since. Of course, there are many I know who have never been released, and (to be honest) they were always the people I knew would never, ever say the words of conversion.

Practice

Finally, there is the issue of practice. Christians in Iraq always practise their faith. There is no concept of being a "nominal" Christian as there is in the West. If you are a Christian you go to church each week (which for Christians in Iraq happens on Fridays and Sundays) and at every festival. Christians take days off work or school for key holy days and, as a result, the fact that they are practising Christians is easily noticed. They do many things differently from the Muslim majority, so there can be no hiding. Everyone knows who the Christians are in their community, which can make things very difficult and dangerous for believers. Nevertheless, our people refuse to deny the practice of their faith.

Our faith is under violent attack here. What is most disturbing about our situation is the fact that this violence is carried out in God's name. Religion has indeed gone "very wrong" here. But then, I acknowledge the fact that almost every religion has been guilty of committing violence in God's name. The most awful example of this is the Holocaust. This was not a Christian undertaking, nor was it done in the name of Christ, but it happened in the heart of Christian Europe and most Christians of all denominations did nothing while millions were sent to be slaughtered in their midst. There were a few who objected and suffered the same terrible death. We can never forget what the Lutheran pastor and theologian Martin Niemöller reportedly told representatives of the Confessing Church in Frankfurt on 6 January 1946:

> *They came first for the Communists,*
> *And I didn't speak up because I wasn't a*
> *Communist.*
> *Then they came for the trade unionists,*
> *And I didn't speak up because I wasn't a trade*
> *unionist.*
> *Then they came for the Jews,*
> *And I didn't speak up because I wasn't a Jew.*
> *Then they came for me,*
> *And by that time no one was left to speak up.*

These are words that challenge us to the core. They remind us that none of us are beyond guilt and that all of us are capable of doing the most awful things.

In God's name

The fact that most of the violence in Iraq has been perpetrated by Muslims does not mean we are against every Muslim – far from it. None of my Muslim friends would ever consider killing or doing anything unlawful in God's name. The sad fact is that some Muslims feel justified in persecuting others simply because they are "infidels". They see Christians as such, first, because they do not recognize Mohammed as the last and greatest of God's prophets. (In truth, not only do my people see him as irrelevant to them, but they believe that to accept him would be a denial of their faith in Jesus as God's Anointed. They do, of course, accept Islam's four other prophets: Nuh [Noah], Ibrahim [Abraham], Musa [Moses] and Isa [Jesus] Himself.)

Second, Christians are often accused of having connections with the West and thus not being properly Iraqi. The fact that our faith originated in the Middle East is not known to many Muslims – whereas I have been fascinated to learn from some of the young people in St George's that they didn't even know there were Christians in the West! When the Americans arrived in 2003 they were amazed to see that some of the soldiers wore crosses. One man even told me he had thought there were Christians only in Iraq. In contrast, many of the Muslim terrorists see everything about the West as Christian – and wrong. Its promiscuity, its general liberalism and its lack of virtue are understood as Christian phenomena. And it is Christians who, in the eyes of many, attacked Iraq in 2003. Some have even compared the invasion to the Crusades.

It is traumatic enough when any of your people are

kidnapped and killed, but when it is some of your own staff, it is particularly difficult. In the summer of 2008, one of my two lay pastors, Majid, was abducted from his house. When his family fled to the church, his house was taken over by the militia involved. His kidnappers contacted us and demanded $60,000 – it was an "economic" rather than a "political" kidnapping. It was a sum of money we simply did not have. We bargained with them and eventually agreed to hand over $40,000. In cases like this, you have to pay up quickly or the hostage is killed quickly. In due course, deeply traumatized, Majid was released and reunited with his wife and three petrified children, and they all moved into our church compound. Majid told us how, throughout his detention, he continually quoted Scripture. His kidnappers constantly told him they wanted to kill him, but they did not. We were all grateful that he had been returned to us alive. Immediately, he and his family began making plans to leave the country, since they had lost everything – even their house had been taken from them. Soon they fled to Syria. Two years later, it looks as though the UN will allow them to enter the USA as "refugees".

Soon after Majid and his family had gone, we had a meeting of the council that represents both my congregations – the one at St George's and the one at the American Embassy chapel. There was only one thing on the agenda: how could we make sure our other pastor, Faiz, wasn't kidnapped? I was acutely aware of how different this discussion was from the business of any church council meeting in the West. The people from the US Army explained that Faiz must not allow any of his movements between home and church to become predictable.

In the end, however, there was only one conclusion we could reach: in reality, there was nothing anyone could do to ensure his safety, except to turn from the natural to the spiritual realm and ask the Lord to protect him.

This is always the best response when our faith is under attack. There is no systematic approach that can minimize the risks, since we cannot change our enemies' perception of us, nor can we neglect our own proclamation and practice of our faith. These things are crucial to our obedience to the God who has promised never to leave us or forsake us. In the midst of all our difficulties, we know without doubt that He is the only way through them. We remember that He told us that our faith will come under attack and that, as the day of His return draws closer, the attacks will only get worse. Indeed, we take heart from the fact that we are under attack, because we believe – we know – that it means we are trusted by our Lord to persevere.

And we will.

6

Loss and Gain

As I have said often, I never underestimate the importance or difficulty of ministry in the West. I also readily acknowledge that I would now not be particularly good at life and ministry in the UK. I used to love my work when I was based in Battersea Rise and Balham Hill, but I don't think I could cope with it now – or that the parishioners could easily cope with me! So says my wife, Caroline, and I'm sure she is right.

I remember when the well-known BBC journalist Michael Buerk was interviewing me for his radio programme *The Choice*. He asked me, rather controversially, if I was not just a "war junkie". I had to stop and think for a moment, since I had never heard the term before. Like most people, I wish that war was a thing of the past, but I have spent a fair amount of time in war zones and confess that war does not frighten me personally – though I have had my fill of the trauma and devastation it causes. Nonetheless, the people of St George's have become my people and so their pain has become my pain and their fear has become my fear. I may not worry about myself, but I do worry about them. I know that they are frequently scared, have no freedom, no security, and are continually targeted simply because they love the Lord Jesus. Life here is replete with losses, but we also experience many gains to counteract them.

Personal loss

Despite nearly always being positive and loving what I do, I recognize that my commitment comes at a price and I have suffered personal loss in many different ways. The greatest loss is that I do not see my family very often. I try to make sure that I spend time with my wife and my boys every month, but it is not easy. As I write I am flying to speak in Dallas, Texas. I returned from Baghdad to London three weeks ago, but I was in England for only one day before I had to fly to America. My schedule has been extremely hectic recently – nine flights in just three weeks. Soon I will be on my way back to England again to spend just one precious day with Caroline and the boys before returning to Baghdad. I do not like being away from them so much. In 2003, I dreamed of a day when they would be able to come to Iraq with me, but that day has not come yet and there is no sign of it coming any time soon.

Another burden is the very reason I am currently on my way to America: I have to raise the funds needed to cover all our expenses in Iraq. It is not easy. I remember the time when I needed just $600 a year to run St George's. Now I need around $175,000 each month to keep things going. In Baghdad, people come to church not only for the worship but also for food, health care and education. We have to deal with all their emergencies. We do, and we rejoice in doing so. When members of my team are killed, as many have been, we have a commitment to keep to their families. There is no social welfare system in Iraq! We continue to provide for them all. Not only do we have to meet the costs of our church and its clinic, with a staff of several doctors, dentists, pharmacists and technicians, we also support many other churches and institutions in Baghdad.

My other great loss is that of my personal freedom. I live my life surrounded by soldiers and police. My security team, which is provided by the Iraqi government, seems to get larger all the time. They are with me from the moment I land at the airport in Baghdad and stay until they return me to the airport several weeks later. There are people watching me every minute of every day. Even when I go to the bathroom they are there! If I have to leave my room in the middle of the night, they are there. I sometimes wish I could escape and live "normally", but despite wishing I could be allowed a little more liberty, I acknowledge that they do a wonderful job and I consider each of them a friend.

Naturally, there are times when I feel like a prisoner. I have tried on several occasions to walk outside the church compound, just to look at the secure road and the compound from the outside, but I have never been allowed. I can venture out only with hordes of armed men around me and in an armour-plated car. How often I wish I could just walk a few yards to the Tigris and pray on the riverbank as I used to – but there is no chance! When I lived in the Green Zone, I used to go regularly to pray by the river, until I was prohibited even from doing that by the Western security firm that looked after me in those days. But it was, I admit, becoming rather traumatic, seeing the increasing number of human bodies bobbing up and down in the water.

I am actually very glad that I now live outside the international zone, in what the Americans call the "Red Zone". The restrictions here are nothing compared to what I had to put up with during the four years I lived in the Green Zone. Then, my church members had to come to services every Saturday. Most often we met in the offices of the Prime Minister or the National Security Adviser, my friend Dr Mowaffak al-Rubaie. Church members would have to queue for hours to pass through all the checkpoints and then queue to get out again. They were difficult days and not all who wanted to come and worship were able to do so – everyone had to wait and come when it was their turn. The same applied when we met each week with our Coalition church members in the one Green Zone hotel – al-Rashid. At other times we met in restaurants or even in the security compound where I lived. So I rejoice that I now live in the Red Zone and nearly 2,000 of our members can gather weekly at St George's. In theory we are in the unprotected area of Baghdad, but I often say that the principal difference between the Green Zone and the Red Zone is that in the former you are attacked from above by rockets, while in the latter you are attacked from below by bombs.

So, my losses are real but, to be honest, they cannot compare with my gains. I share life here with the most wonderful people who are like family to me. They are not like parishioners or members of a congregation, they are my people – my people whom I love and who love me. We may live amidst violence and terror, but we have such peace because our God is so real to us. We may have lost everything but we have not lost our Lord. We live in His love and are constantly aware of

His presence. I do not mean just that we know intellectually that He is with us; I mean that we experience His physical presence. His presence is a reality we can shelter in daily.

God's healing presence

One of the main ways in which God's presence is tangibly felt and visibly seen here is through a demonstration of His healing power. I have always believed strongly in the power of God to heal and in England I would often conduct healing services. But the reality was, sometimes people were healed and often they were not. I have witnessed something very different here in Iraq – healing on a completely different level. Here in Baghdad we pray regularly for people to be healed. I have already mentioned that St George's has a large and successful medical clinic, which can treat a wide variety of illnesses. The vast majority of our patients are not Christians and part of our purpose is to show them the healing love of Jesus. If our medical staff cannot do anything for someone, however, they send them to us in the church for prayer. Here, prayer for healing is not just sometimes effective – it nearly always is. Here, in the midst of brokenness, we see the healing power of God. We have a Lord who always meets with those in need. Whether that is by imparting total restoration or total peace, it always happens.

I am a fairly traditional Anglican priest and not someone who considers himself to have a great "gift of healing", but here I am continually seeing people healed after prayer. We have seen not just sick people made well, but even the dead raised.

Members of the Mothers' Union at St George's regularly visit people at home or in hospital, and recently when they went to one ward they found a woman there crying bitterly. When they asked her what was wrong, she told them her baby had died. Our women went to the mortuary and found the little thing lying cold and lifeless. They prayed for him and within a few minutes the baby started to cry. When they took him back to his mother, her tears of grief were turned to tears of joy. This experience of healing is one of the reasons for the incredible growth of our church. People know that at St George's things happen! Despite our losses we have gained so much.

Wheels within wheels

Another of our "gains" has been the visible presence of angels. I had read of angels in the Bible, of course, and I, and others, had regularly prayed for their protection in Iraq. But until three years ago I had never actually seen one. Towards the end of 2007, quite suddenly, we started to see angelic forms. They look very much like we expect angels to look – like males with wings – but they are strange figures, large and translucent. We take them seriously.

Occasionally, we also see strange images appearing around the place that look like wheels within wheels. We have actually taken photographs of these and some of them appear in this book. At times, these wheels (that can at times appear like blobs) are so prolific that it is difficult to take pictures because they are everywhere. I have tried many different cameras, but the results are always the same. We do not understand what these images are, but we regard them as a sign of the presence of the Spirit of God. We are in the same land that the prophet Ezekiel was in when he saw something similar, as the first chapter of his book records:

> *As I looked at the living creatures, I saw a wheel on the ground beside each creature with its four faces. This was the appearance and structure of the wheels. They sparkled like chrysolite, and all four looked alike. Each appeared to be made like a wheel intersecting a wheel. As they moved, they would go in any one of the four directions the creatures faced; the wheels did not turn about as the creatures went. Their rims were high and awesome, and all four rims were full of eyes all around.*
>
> *When the living creatures moved, the wheels beside them moved; and when the living creatures rose from the ground, the wheels also rose. Wherever the spirit would go, they would go, and the wheels would rise along with them, because the spirit of the living creatures was in the wheels. When the creatures moved, they also moved; when the creatures stood still, they also stood still; and when the creatures rose from the ground, the wheels rose along with them, because the spirit of the living creatures was in the wheels.*

Ezekiel 1:15–21

So, Ezekiel saw some very peculiar things and so do we. He knew they were signs that came from the Almighty and this is how we interpret what we see. They appear only in St George's and some other churches in Iraq and in other places of great spiritual significance such as Ezekiel's tomb in El Kifl, just north of Najaf. We do not understand what they are, but they assure us that the Lord is with us here in the fire.

The fruit of the Spirit

Apart from the healings and the presence of the angelic among us, another "gain" we experience is an unusual abundance of the fruit of the Spirit. I have never seen such love, joy and peace in the midst of so much tragedy. I talk constantly about the love I experience at St George's because it is so tangible, but so is the joy, despite the terror and violence that surround us. At the heart of our church is amazing joy, not just in theory but in practice. The joy of the Lord is indeed our strength. Yes, we cry and grieve – and often despair – when our people are injured or killed, but we soon return to joy. Maybe our joy is a type of survival mechanism, but it is real and substantive nonetheless. It means that even living in the shadow of terror, we are not a sad people.

The third fruit of the Spirit is also so important to us: peace. When St George's was reopened in 2003, I preached on the words that are engraved in the ruins of the old Coventry cathedral:

> *"The glory of this present house will be greater than the glory of the former house," says the Lord Almighty. "And in this place I will grant peace," declares the Lord Almighty.*

> Haggai 2:9

Back then, I had such hope for a peace that was going to be achieved through political change. Iraq was so different after the war: there was a new freedom that no one there had experienced before. But it did not last long. It was only a matter of weeks before the violence was escalating rapidly. In place of people's great fear of Saddam Hussein's regime a new dread emerged – the dread of chaos and destruction. I remember kneeling in the church and asking God: "Why are things so awful? Why have our hopes been destroyed?"

And yet, all the time, our church grew bigger and bigger, even as the situation grew worse. Then, one day as I was walking around the compound, it suddenly dawned on me that this was indeed a place of incredible peace. This past year, Lord Hylton said the same to me after a service at St George's. He told me that here he had "experienced peace as never before". As God had promised: "In this place I will grant peace."

We have indeed lost much but we have also gained more than I could ever have imagined possible.

7

WHEN MY BODY FAILS

I n Chapter 2 I mentioned that I have MS. For the first seven years after my diagnosis in 1998 I managed fairly well, and there was only one period in all that time when I was too ill to go to work. That was in 2003 when I had my first injection of beta interferon, which was then thought to be the only treatment available for MS. My condition had been deteriorating and this drug was supposed to arrest the development of the illness. I was not living in the right area to get it free on the National Health Service, so a friend raised the money for me to buy it at a cost of over $1,000 a month for three injections per week. But when I had my first injection, almost immediately I began to feel considerably worse.

Within hours, my skin was turning red and I was swelling up. The next day I continued to deteriorate, so I went to see my neurologist. He was very concerned about my state and said that I was obviously allergic to the drug and must not take it again. I followed his instructions, and within days I was feeling well enough to return to work. But now I had to face the fact that the only known treatment for MS was not available to me. The future was not looking good.

Around this time I was asked to conduct the funeral of a friend of mine whom I had first met in hospital five years before, at the time when he and I were both diagnosed with MS. The disease had killed him, whereas I was still alive, though I now felt much worse than I had felt back then. Meanwhile, I had people coming to pray for me, or wanting to pray with me, all the time. This was often very difficult. I was made to feel bad for not getting better. It often seemed that I and my supposed lack of belief were being held to blame, or else it was to do with my family or my heritage. The truth is that I trusted totally in my God and never doubted that He could heal me – but it simply did not happen. It got to the point where I really didn't want people to pray with me any more.

The whole experience was so painful that it has deeply influenced how I pray with people today. I will never portray someone's illness as their fault. I never doubt that God can heal, because I know that He can, when and how He wants to. I also know that there are times when someone who is ill does not have the faith that God will heal them, and sometimes they do not even want to be healed. Such situations call for sensitivity and wisdom. Often our prayers should be said privately, not in the presence of the person concerned, asking God to make them sincerely open to receiving the healing touch of Jesus before we ever try to pray for them publicly.

Unlike most people with MS, hot weather does not make my condition worse. In fact, it makes it better, for which I am grateful. This meant that for a long while, at least, I was able to continue my work in the Middle East. But by 2005 I had deteriorated so much that I was feeling ill most of the time and whenever I returned to England I was having to spend nearly all my time in bed. Nevertheless, I was determined to keep going. I managed to keep all my speaking appointments and to find enough strength for each one. People would often remark that it was good that I was able to be at home with my family, but it wasn't good, because I always felt so awful when I was there. I would invariably get ill within a day of going home.

Caroline could see that I was getting worse and that being in the UK did not agree with me. We therefore decided that the family would meet me in Israel the next time I was due back from Iraq, and we would try to have some time together there. Even that didn't work, however; I felt even worse than I had in England. Privately, Caroline came to the conclusion that holidays with me must now be a thing of the past. If ever I stopped work, my health always declined sharply. It was as if I could keep the disease in check only by working continually. Even in Iraq, however, I was now feeling very unwell all the time.

When the time came to move on from my post at Coventry Cathedral, my doctor told me that I was now too ill to work in the Church of England, as indeed I was. By this stage we had established the Foundation for Relief and Reconciliation in the Middle East (FRRME), and it was decided that this was the body that I should work for henceforth. Caroline and I moved to a house in Hampshire in the south of England, where her late grandparents had once lived and which now belonged to her parents. It was the first house we had ever lived in together that was not church-owned. I did what little I could to help with the move and then returned to

Iraq to resume my work combating religious sectarianism and running both St George's and the Anglican chapel in Saddam's old Republican Palace, which was then still the Coalition headquarters.

I was also, beside this increasing workload, still responsible for the Alexandria Process (widely regarded as the religious "track" of the Middle East Peace Process) and so I was often in Israel/Palestine, though by 2008 I had to give up this side of my work as things in Iraq intensified.

A glimpse of light

My health continued to go downhill. When I was not in meetings (which, admittedly, I was most of the time), I was lying on my bed in a small trailer in the Green Zone. In December 2008, an Iraqi friend came to see me. Dr Abdel Majid Hammadi was professor of haematology at Baghdad (formerly Saddam) Medical City, the biggest teaching hospital in Iraq. I had been working with him for several years, even before the invasion in 2003, and had helped him to set up Iraq's first-ever bone marrow transplant centre. He had visited me twice in Coventry and on one of those occasions had brought over key members of his team for six weeks' training at the Birmingham Children's Hospital.

When he came into my trailer, he told me he had come to see me because he intended to make me better. I had heard this so many times before, usually from doctors who wanted a lot of money, and I had tried so many different remedies and none of them worked. I asked Dr Majid what he proposed, and he said he had looked up multiple sclerosis on the

Internet, and what I needed was stem cell treatment. I had heard a lot about the high hopes people had of this, and I had also heard about the serious ethical concerns, as many of the stem cells used are taken from embryos or umbilical cords. I asked him what exactly he had in mind and he explained that he wanted to inject some of my own stem cells into the space between the vertebrae in my lower back. I asked him whether he had done this before, and he said no. He explained that I would need injections for three days prior to the treatment to increase my white blood cells, then my stem cells would be extracted by machine.

I agreed to give this a go, since I had little to lose, and it was decided that this should be done after Christmas, after I had spent a few days with my family in Hampshire. (I always go home for Christmas, as that festival is bigger in the UK than in Iraq. For the same reason, I always celebrate Easter in Baghdad.) I duly flew to England and prayed hard that I would be well enough to enjoy the festivities with Caroline and the boys. I was not. It was only a matter of hours after returning to England that I became so ill that I had to go to bed. It is difficult to describe how bad I felt. It was not just a matter of being poorly – I found it hard even to speak. Being unable to join in at such a happy time, I felt very isolated and alone. The festivities were happening around me but I felt far away. Someone said to me, "Just pray and you will be all right," but I felt too ill even to pray.

I returned to Iraq still feeling terrible. Arrangements were made with an Iraqi government minister to take me to hospital for the treatment, and I was transported there in the usual armour-plated vehicle accompanied by heavy security. I had not seen the hospital for several years and was shocked to find it so dilapidated and dirty. I was relieved to think that my procedure was going to be done in the bone marrow transplant unit, which had to be clean (and was). Dr Majid and his staff connected me up to a machine that took blood out of my left arm, spun it in a centrifuge to extract the stem cells and then put it back into my right arm. It took about two hours to collect 25 cc of stem cells. Just as the process was coming to an end, Dr Majid remarked that I had bought this machine for the unit. I had indeed helped to set up the unit a few years previously, but I had no idea that I had been responsible for getting this particular piece of equipment! After another hour, Dr Majid carried out the lumbar puncture very expertly, and then I returned to my cabin in the Green Zone.

The pain from the puncture was severe and kept me on my bed for most of the following week, but after only five hours I knew that my condition was going to improve greatly. The feeling of nausea subsided, my speech was much better and in due course I could move around much more freely. After two weeks, I flew to England and this time I didn't at once feel worse. Caroline could see the difference immediately. She noticed that my whole temperament had changed and she summed up the situation by saying this was the nicest I had ever been!

I returned to Iraq a different man. Dr Majid was overjoyed. I had been his guinea pig and he was already treating other patients who were seeing the same kind of success. I paid another visit to his unit, but this time the stem cells were injected into my soft tissue so that there were no side-effects. The third time, a neurosurgeon did an injection into my cervical vertebrae. Each time since then I have had the injections in different places to try to treat different symptoms. As I write, I have just had my nineteenth treatment – in the soft tissue near to my brain stem to try to deal with my residual problems of balance.

The land of healing

I have thanked God continually that, although I never expected much from this treatment, for the first time ever I have been getting better and not worse. It was only after I started receiving these injections that I realized just how ill I had become. Now, one and a half years later, I feel totally different from before. I no longer regard myself as ill, even though I am conscious that there are things that are still difficult for me to do. And every time I go to the hospital, in my armour-plated car surrounded by soldiers, it never ceases to amaze me that it is only here, in violence-torn Baghdad, that I have been able to actually get better.

Dr Majid and his close colleague Dr Saad have so far treated over 1,000 people, suffering not only from MS but also from cerebral palsy, muscular dystrophy, Parkinson's disease, motor neurone disease and many other conditions including spinal cord injuries and irreparable fractures. As well as Baghdad, they now have a clinic in Arbil, in the safety of Kurdistan. Their patients are mainly Iraqi, but some have come from other Arab countries – and the treatment has also been given to American patients in Lebanon. These two doctors, who were originally haematologists, are now specialists in auto-stem-cell treatment. Basically, they are treating people who were considered untreatable, who had no hope – and many of them have shown radical improvement.

As I began to get better, I still found one thing distressing – the knowledge that there are hundreds and thousands of people whose conditions could be treated in this way, and yet who live without that hope. Throughout the rest of the world scientists have been researching and researching the use of stem cells, while here in Baghdad Dr Majid and Dr Saad have just got on with treating people – and it has worked. I have also been very annoyed with the attitude of many of the drug companies, which have been partly to blame for this very cheap treatment not being widely adopted. Is it not a gift of God – delivered in the very land where the Garden of Eden used to be? As someone has said, our healing is within us!

I have already remarked that were it not for my illness, it is doubtful whether I would even be in Iraq. Yet it is here that I have found a measure of healing for this illness, and it is enabling me to continue the work God has given me. Is it not so that sometimes God moves through adverse circumstances and even sickness when we will not cooperate with Him in health and tranquillity? But once again I have proven that He who has called me will not fail me.

8

BEARING THE HEAT

Every day in Baghdad we are aware of the "heat" we endure. Every day we are aware of how much our people, including me, are suffering. Because of this, there is one characteristic of our existence here that is more prominent than any other: we can never worry about tomorrow, we just live for today. The "heat" we bear is as real and oppressive as the physical temperature (which recently reached a scalding 58°C and only dropped a few degrees at night!). We live with constant uncertainty; we are surrounded by violence, war, tragedy and the continual possibility of those we love being snatched from us. But though there are many difficulties, there are many positives that keep us going. In Chapter 6 I explored the downside as well as the upside of life in Baghdad. Now I want to stop and examine what it is really like ministering here in the heat, and how one keeps going when things are so tough.

There is a saying in Arabic: "*Yom asal, yom basal*", which means, "One day honey, one day onions" and speaks of the bittersweet quality of life. I used to designate my days as one or the other of these – a honey day or an onion day – and certainly, a good day was frequently followed by a bad one!

But eventually I changed my perspective. I decided to believe that every day was going to be good. This was more than a philosophical shift – it was a spiritual shift – a deliberate act of the will to focus on Jesus and the promises of God, as the Bible encourages us to do. Now, I continually refer to positive, faith-filled scriptures, and this encourages me and gives me hope, even in the fire. I would like us to examine some of these verses.

Perfect love

The verse that is most important to me is 1 John 4:18: "Perfect love drives out fear." What I love about this verse is that before it even mentions fear it speaks about love. It presents the solution before the problem. I do not fear much, but I talk constantly about love. When my people are afraid, I tell them that they are loved – loved by God and loved by everyone in our community. It is simply love that sustains us and keeps us going. So often in books and sermons we are told about the importance of love in our faith, but to us in Iraq love is a matter of life or death. We experience the reality of the love that surrounds us, enables us, and sustains us through the heat of the fire.

Similarly, in 2 Timothy 1:7 we read that "God has not given us a spirit of fear, but of power and of love and of a sound mind." So, with love goes strength and power – the power to persevere through the heat of the fire and the power to do what others may consider impossible. It is this kind of love that can enable all Christians to deal with the difficulties they encounter, even in the safety of the West. It is a love that will always prevent fear from taking control of us. At times, things may seem impossible: how will we accomplish the tasks that we need to, which are often so immense? Jesus gave us the answer: "What is impossible with men is possible with God" (Luke 18:27).

In Iraq, there is so much that seems impossible, but for God all things are possible. For us at St George's, these are not just nice, comforting words from the Bible; this is how we live our lives. There are times when we all wonder how we are going to do what has to be done and it would be very easy to think that we simply can't go on – the heat is just too much to bear. Then we remember that we are not alone in our difficulties; we do not have to bear them on our own. The apostle Paul endured many similar difficulties. He knew, as I have known, what it is like to face the challenge of ministry with a constant "thorn in my flesh". Paul pleaded with our Lord to remove his thorn, but God's answer to him was simply, "My grace is sufficient for you, for my power is made perfect in weakness" (2 Corinthians 12:9).

Like Paul, I often feel weak and inadequate to meet the challenges set before me, but I remember that God's power is indeed expressed perfectly through my weakness. There are times when I simply do not know what to say – not in church, usually, but in my other work, such as when I am trying to engage with religious sectarianism. Sometimes a meeting is so intense, so difficult, that I simply cry out to God for help. The Holy Spirit promises to come to our aid and give us the words to say during such times, and indeed that has been my experience. Countless times I have had no idea what to say and silently, in my heart, I have cried out to God and He has heard me and has given me the right words.

I cannot pretend that I do not feel the heat – I do, and it can be very painful, but I have to find a way through it. I cannot hold on to the pain I experience, but always determine to release it to the Lord. I never want pain to be the factor that governs my attitudes. I remember the problems that people used to bring to me when I was ministering in England. Even if I sometimes feel a bit impatient with the concerns of suburbia now, I have to acknowledge that they were all real problems and the people who faced them felt real pain. Indeed, as I look back on my own life, I realize that the greatest pain I have gone through myself was not in Iraq but in the safety of Britain. One can never underestimate the severity of mental pain or depression. It does not matter where you are when sheer darkness envelops you. There are some people at St George's who suffer this degree of despair, depression and loss, and all we can do is what anyone anywhere else would do: pray for them, be there for them, and surround them with love.

However, when your faith is in the fire, the reality of God's presence is always evident. God's presence amongst our little leadership team at St George's and the strength that it gives us are so real that they prevent us from slipping into despair. We are surrounded by brokenness, uncertainty and tragedy, but we know we cannot hold on to them. We find ways to leave the pain behind us. This is what the truths contained in these scriptures do – they prevent us from allowing pain to determine our attitudes.

The role of suffering

In Philippians 1:29–30 we read:

> *For it has been granted to you on behalf of Christ*
> *not only to believe on him, but also to suffer for*
> *him, since you are going through the same struggle*
> *you saw I had, and now hear that I still have.*

We see suffering as an essential part of our service to our Lord. Just as Paul suffered for his faith, so we are called to suffer for ours. We do not like to suffer, but we know that it is part of our calling: we are told to take up our cross and follow Him, and this we do.

By doing this we are heeding the advice of the apostle Peter, who wrote:

> *But how is it to your credit if you receive a*
> *beating for doing wrong and endure it? But if you*
> *suffer for doing good and you endure it, this is*
> *commendable before God. To this you were called,*
> *because Christ suffered for you, leaving you an*
> *example, that you should follow in his steps*
>
> 1 Peter 2:20–21

Here in Iraq we are living examples of this and see ourselves as following in the footsteps of our Lord and Master. Scriptures such as these are not very popular – and many people would view them as terrifying and sombre. But far from being miserable, we are full of joy! As I have said many times, the congregation of St George's are the most joyful people I have ever served.

This brings me to the biblical concept of joy in suffering. The reason why we rejoice, even in the midst of pain, is because "we know that in all things God works for the good of those who love him, who have been called according to his purpose" (Romans 8:28). God can turn around for our good even the most terrible things. We do not believe that the pain will last forever. We know without doubt that these words are true:

> *Weeping may endure for a night,*
> *But joy comes in the morning.*
>
> Psalm 30:5 NKJV

We are quite prepared for that joy to be the joy of heaven, because it is never far from the mind of any of us here in Baghdad that "soon and very soon, we are going to see the King". The fact that our ultimate destination is heaven is central to our life and being. This certainty is only strengthened by the signs we constantly see around us and by our awareness that we are in the very country where the history of human salvation began, with Abraham.

So though we are in the heat, we are continually blessed and encouraged by God's word. Time and again it resonates with our suffering. In the church in other parts of the world, such passages are often mentioned only in passing, but to us they are the "oil" that keeps us functioning. The promises of God allow us to release our pain to Him and keep moving forward in the joy of serving the King. They help us to bear the heat and look positively to the future, despite the opposition that faces us. There cannot be any such word as "can't" here in Iraq. We have to persevere, and we do. And in everything we see the glory of God.

9

THE PRESENCE OF THE ALMIGHTY

When things are bad here in Baghdad it is always a temptation to allow oneself to spiral into despair or fear. During such times I am challenged to remain in God's presence. From the place of His presence I respond to circumstances very differently – not from an earthly, emotional perspective, but from a supernatural one. When I think about living in God's presence it means three specific things to me that I want to discuss in this chapter:

* It is about living "in His glory".
* It is about the presence and guidance of His Holy Spirit.
* It is about the gifts that God gives us to accomplish His will on earth.

The glory of God

People often ask me why I always talk about the glory of God more than I do about His kingdom. To me, the glory of God is an inseparable part of the kingdom of God. It is God's glorious, physical presence that we need to experience more than anything else in our lives, because it is His presence that empowers us for effective service. The more time we spend in God's presence, the more we experience His miraculous power. The more time we spend immersed in His love and exposed to His glory, the more we are able to love others.

When Christians speak about "the glory of God" they are usually referring to His Shekinah glory. Shekinah is a Hebrew word, more properly pronounced she-heenah, which means "to settle, inhabit or dwell" (see Exodus 40:35, for example, where the glory of the Lord "filled" the Tabernacle). In other words, God dwells or rests in a place or upon a person. Shekinah is also a feminine word and is often used when Jews welcome the Sabbath (Shabbat) "like a bride", as something beautiful and special. It was also the term used by the high priest to describe the likeness of the holy of holies when he entered it once a year on Yom Kippur (the Day of Atonement). This was the place where God was seen to "dwell", and the high priest would spend a whole week purifying himself as he prepared to go into the very presence of the Almighty.

To be truthful, I did not expect that I would ever see any real, tangible evidence of the glory of God in Iraq – having been exposed time and again to the evil that exists in this place. But I began to catch glimpses of it after the war in 2003 and eventually I came to see and experience more and more of God's glory, evidenced through many healings and miracles, some of which I have already mentioned.

I was amazed that God's glory could manifest itself in such extraordinary ways here in Iraq, but that changed the day I heard God tell me to study the entire book of Ezekiel.

Not long afterwards I met a lady at the Hebrew University in Jerusalem who was an expert on both the Aramaic language and the book of Ezekiel. She was not an Israeli but an African American, called (unusually) Albert. I learned so much from her! I shared with her how I had seen so much of God's glory manifested in Iraq, but couldn't explain why this should be the case. She, however, didn't think it strange at all – and she provided me with an explanation.

She showed me very clearly from Scripture that the glory of God had gone to Babylon with the people of Israel in the Second Exile and, according to the opening verses of Ezekiel 43, it would return to the temple in Jerusalem from the east, through the east gate of Jerusalem. Where is the glory today? "It is to the east of Jerusalem," she told me, "in Iraq." I had never heard this before, but it makes perfect sense to me now. I can testify to the fact that His glory is residing here. God's presence is tangible, real, visible and awe-inspiring.

I never dreamed that I would see God's glory in the ways I have done here. I had encountered God's presence in a deep way before – such as the time I recalled at the beginning of this book, when God first called me into His service and which had a major impact on my life at the time. But here, in the heat of the fire, I have experienced God's presence to an altogether different magnitude. It seems to me that the more dire the situation we find ourselves in, the more God is willing to manifest His presence. He reveals Himself to us in such a way that His presence overwhelms and diminishes our present troubles. All of our people at St George's testify to this. In our main services every Friday and Sunday, we always have a time when I ask people to tell me what has happened to them over the past week. As they share their stories I regularly hear two things: one is how they or their loved ones have been affected by the violence, and the other is the glorious ways in which God has intervened in their lives. These stories are always deeply moving. They tell tale after tale of the manifestation of the glory of God.

I have already mentioned the numerous healings we have experienced and the angels we have seen, so let me tell you about another phenomenon. According to the book of Joel,

> *I will pour out my Spirit on all people.*
> *Your sons and daughters will prophesy,*
> *your old men will dream dreams,*
> *your young men will see visions.*
> *Even on my servants, both men and women,*
> *I will pour out my Spirit in those days.*
> *I will show wonders in the heavens*
> *and on the earth,*
> *blood and fire and billows of smoke.*
> *The sun will be turned to darkness…*
>
> Joel 2:28–31

Here, I hear stories about God speaking to people in dreams all the time. People have dreams where they are instructed not to do something they were intending to do or are told to do something that they would not normally do. Often Jesus appears in these dreams, giving instructions; and often, so does His mother, Mary. An emphasis on the Virgin Mary has never been a part of my tradition. I have always held her in the highest regard and have often preached about her, but her veneration has never been a part of my spiritual life. But I have been deeply challenged by her continual appearance to my people during what are clearly genuine encounters with the Almighty. Many testify to the fact that they would not be alive today if they had not done what the Virgin Mary told them to do in a dream. All I can say in response to this is that I am willing to learn from them as they are willing to learn from me – since dreams are such a fundamental aspect of the lives of my people.

Since we live in such a dangerous place, people will often dream that they should avoid a certain place on a certain day – not to go to a particular market, for example, or not to take their child to school on a certain day. They heed the warning and, sure enough, on that day a terrorist attack takes place in the very location where they or their child would have been, and their lives are saved. At other times, people say that they have had a vision of the Lord, or have seen a strange vision of the cloud of His glory. The Bible often describes God's presence in this way and seeing this cloud is not uncommon – I have seen it myself. In fact, I first came to terms with the presence of God's glory here in Baghdad when I saw the cloud hovering over the Tigris. Just as a cloud led the children of Israel by day in the wilderness, so too we see God's glory in a cloud, and it reassures us that He is present here with us.

The Holy Spirit

The second aspect of God's presence is that of the power and presence of His Holy Spirit. It is not easy to separate our awareness of the glory of God from the presence of His Spirit, and so I tend to think of the latter as a constant awareness of

God's guidance and comfort. It takes time to learn to recognize God's voice speaking to us (just as it did for the prophet Samuel when he was a young boy) and to be aware of when He is directing us. But eventually we can attune ourselves to the Holy Spirit's promptings and guidance. Certainly I sometimes make mistakes, but as time goes on, I make far fewer than I used to. It is essential that we learn to hear, and listen, when God speaks.

I have mentioned earlier how often I ask for, and wait for, the direction of the Holy Spirit – for example, when I am in a difficult meeting. There are times when I genuinely do not know what to say, particularly when dealing with some complex religious sectarian issue. When I am sitting across the table from some really bad people, people who are directly involved in killing, it is through the intervention of the Holy Spirit that the words to say always come to me. God always speaks – often with words that I would logically not have chosen myself. How does this happen in practice? The Holy Spirit forms the words He wants us to speak in our mind. He may also speak to us through a simple phrase that someone else speaks, which acts as a catalyst to produce the words we are meant to say. The Holy Spirit can even use music or some other form of media to intervene. In the past, when I have found myself wondering how to respond to a complicated situation, I have heard someone talking on the TV in the background about something totally unrelated and have known immediately, "That's what I should say!"

Rarely does God make us wait for important answers. His Holy Spirit desires to equip us for every situation. I continually meet people in the West who tell me that they are "waiting on God" for answers to various situations. I confess that I often get rather annoyed with them! It is not their fault, of course, but I have become used to hearing God's answers very quickly, and therefore anticipate and expect an ongoing dialogue with the Holy Spirit on a moment-by-moment basis. When you are in the middle of a war zone, you have to act quickly and you invariably need an answer NOW! In respect of hearing God's voice, my medical emergency training prepared me well. I know what it means to hear an order and follow it immediately.

The gifts of the Spirit

The third aspect of God's presence is the operation of the gifts of the Holy Spirit – the tools God has made available for us to do our work. There are three groups of gifts in the New Testament and each group brings glory to a different Person of the Godhead:

* Romans 12:6–8 lists seven "gifts of faith" – prophesying, serving, teaching, encouraging, contributing to the needs of others, leadership and showing mercy – gifts which glorify God the Father.

* Ephesians 4:11 refers to the equipping of apostles, prophets, evangelists, pastors and teachers – "gifts of action" that glorify God the Son.

* The gifts that especially enable us to carry out our work in the fire are the nine "charismatic gifts" listed in 1 Corinthians 12:7–11, which bring glory to the Holy Spirit: wisdom, knowledge, faith, gifts of healing, miraculous powers, prophecy, the ability to distinguish between spirits, speaking in tongues and the interpretation of tongues.

For us at St George's, living and walking in God's presence means allowing the gifts of the Spirit to work in us and through us on a daily basis. I would like to look at each of these charismatic gifts of 1 Corinthians 12 in turn and briefly mention how they are manifested amongst us.

Wisdom

The gift of wisdom may appear to be less dramatic or less "supernatural" than other gifts, but it is nonetheless essential. Almost every day I am asked to get involved in issues that I do not fully understand and so every day I need the wisdom of the Holy Spirit just to know what I should do. This is particularly so in my non-church work concerning religious sectarianism – work so secret that I cannot say anything about it except that it is very complex. The Holy Spirit is always standing beside me, inspiring and enabling me to say what is needed. I know how real and significant this gift of wisdom is, because in myself I am frequently at a loss to know what to say.

Knowledge

The gift of knowledge is more obviously supernatural. Sometimes God simply tells us something we need to know. One day, when I was leading a service at St George's, I became acutely aware that God was telling me that a particular, smartly dressed man who had just come into the church had to be removed. I had never before had anyone ejected from the church, and there was no obvious reason why this man presented a threat. I didn't know him, but then we often see people at St George's who we do not know. At my request the security guards removed him and handed him over to the

Iraqi army. It was then that it was discovered he was wearing a "suicide belt" packed with explosives. Who knows why he did not detonate it at once? But I was so grateful for God's protection. Scores of people could so easily have been killed.

Happily, as well as intervening in extreme circumstances such as this, the Holy Spirit will also impart knowledge to us concerning more benign matters – such as revealing information about a particular treatment that will make a person well or about the help that a family presently needs.

Discernment

Discernment or the ability to "distinguish between spirits" is the gift that I feel I have most strongly. There are times when this feels definitely supernatural and clearly a gift from the Holy Spirit, and there are other times when it seems entirely natural. Discernment is essentially a matter of identifying whether something or somebody is of God or the evil one. If you are trying to work for peace, you have to engage with those who are causing violent conflict. We cannot (as I often say) only deal with "nice" people. In this context, the gift of discernment is vital, because the Holy Spirit can help us to know whether we can make any headway with these people or not.

I will never forget the day I was meeting in Amman with the High Council of Religious Leaders in Iraq and one of their number, Sheikh Dr Abdel Latif Humayem, kept telling me that a key person was flying in from Syria to meet me. The moment this man entered the room, I felt very strongly that he was evil and that I should not work with him. I was in no doubt that this was discernment given to me by God for that particular moment. I have to say that the man did not look evil – he came across as well educated and at first what he said seemed innocuous – but the more he talked, the more conscious I was that he was evil and there was nothing I could do with him. He then said to me, "Those who cure you will kill you." It was a strange and disturbing phrase and in the end I asked him to leave. Later, I discovered that he was one of al-Qa'ida's leaders in Iraq. That night, I wrote in my spiritual update to my supporters: "I met the devil today." He was hinting, cryptically, that Britain was going to be attacked and indeed, a few weeks later, some Muslim men were arrested for trying to detonate car bombs in London and Glasgow. At least two of them turned out to be doctors.

On another occasion, a lady who was an architect came to see me and brought with her several other members of her family. She was a Muslim, but I immediately felt very positive about them all and was sure God was telling me, "They're mine!" As soon as we had finished discussing our business together, she told me they wanted to talk with me about something else. They then all declared that they loved Jesus and wanted to follow Him. To my surprise, they told me they had already been coming to church and wanted me to baptize them. Secretly, I did so, there in my study, and their joy was immense. Tragically, within a week, they were all in heaven. The news of their baptism had got out and following Jesus had cost them their lives. Nonetheless, I am sure that I did what God told me to do. We must constantly listen to the Holy Spirit and follow our spiritual instincts. Even in the midst of chaos, God can direct us and bring order to what we do.

Praying in and interpreting tongues

Speaking in tongues (or *glossolalia*) has for many years been regarded in charismatic circles as one of the key gifts of the Spirit – a sign that an individual has been "baptized in the Holy Spirit" and filled with the Spirit. I did not have a dramatic conversion experience as some have, but I will never forget the day at St Mark's, Kennington, when I was filled with the Holy Spirit while still a young student at St Thomas'. I went to the altar rail and was prayed for by a wonderful woman called Anthea. I felt the power of God pass through my body and I was released into the gift of tongues. Since then, I have often prayed in tongues and will do so especially when I do not know what to pray – which in Baghdad is frequently. This gives me great encouragement, because when I pray in tongues I feel the closeness of God's presence and am aware that He hears me and responds.

There have been occasions when I have given an interpretation of tongues, but so far this is the only gift that has not been exercised at St George's. There are a few people that I am aware of in my congregation who pray in tongues, but there have never been any messages in tongues during services. One day, perhaps, this gift may become a prominent part of the life of our church, but it will only be when the Holy Spirit decides.

Prophecy

Though few of my congregation would ever claim to be prophets or even claim to exercise the gift of prophecy, it is remarkable how, time after time, people will come to me and tell me what God has said to them. In fact, they are moving in the prophetic without realizing it, since invariably their messages concern me or the church, what we should do and what we should not. They tend to address issues that could seriously affect us and it is obviously God speaking to us.

I remember very clearly the day when I heard the Lord tell me to set up a clinic. The following day, my friend Jonathan Webb, who worked for a security company in Iraq, told me about a Christian clinic he had opened not far away and said we should do the same at St George's. It was a confirmation of what God had said to me the day before. Today, we have the largest and best clinic in Baghdad and it is a wonderful way to demonstrate the love of Jesus. When the Lord speaks to us, we must do what He says! Frequently He will speak first to us and then confirm His will prophetically through others.

Faith

Faith is critical if we are going to serve God effectively. In fact, we need faith simply to survive and live out each day, especially in difficult circumstances. Here I am not simply referring to faith as "belief", but the type of faith that, through prayer, sees mountains move when we need them to in order to accomplish God's purposes. We cannot "work up" faith like this by trying to believe something with all our hearts. Rather, it is birthed out of time spent in God's presence. Our faith is faith in the nature of God – trusting that He is who His word says He is and that He will do what He has promised to do. And He imparts this faith to us as a gift.

I have already mentioned that each month at St George's I somehow have to find around $175,000 to meet the needs of our people. This sum covers the cost of providing food each week for 4,000 people, pays many people's rent, and runs the largest clinic in Baghdad with all its associated costs. Besides this, we have to deal with the frequent "emergencies" that arise – cases where people require surgery or other intensive medical treatment that our clinic cannot provide. Each month this demands the exercise of the gift of faith! We have no reserves, and yet the Lord always provides. He always does – but I wish He didn't always wait until the very last minute! As someone once said, "God is never late, but He rarely takes the opportunity to be early!"

So trusting in God's provision for our needs is one very important aspect of faith. Then it takes faith simply to live one's life in the fire. Wherever we go, there are dangers and whatever we do, there are risks – not just for me, but for all our people. Every Friday and Sunday in St George's I listen as people tell their stories, and they always give credit to God that they have survived another week in Baghdad. We put our faith in the goodness and mercy of God to preserve us.

The miraculous

At every turn we see miracles here. Once again, no individual here would claim miraculous powers, yet God is constantly intervening, working in and through individuals, doing things we could never have expected. For that reason, miracles here are considered the norm rather than the exception. We talk about "living in the miraculous" and we do – as evidenced by the stories told elsewhere in this book.

Healing

Healing, which I have already discussed in Chapter 6, is at the heart of the life of our church – healing to a degree I have not witnessed elsewhere. I have often asked myself why this should be. I have always believed that God can heal miraculously, but before beginning ministry in Iraq I had only ever seen a few people healed. No doubt you will realize that, due to my medical training, I always want to see serious evidence that a person has been healed. I do not pronounce someone "healed" unless I am certain this is actually the case. Sadly, I have seen many people prayed for and told they are healed, when there is no real evidence to support it.

What I have seen in Baghdad, however, has been real and authentic. Many of the healings that take place here are serious and dramatic. I do not wish to minimize anyone's suffering, but these are not people complaining of a vague pain in their shoulder or some similar ailment. Here, people who have been diagnosed with conditions such as chronic renal failure have been touched by God and restored to health. Many of the healings here have taken place in life-or-death situations. Having a clinic in the church compound helps, of course, to deal with minor illnesses. But sometimes, those who are very ill have no other option than prayer. So the clinic sends us patients to pray for and, in turn, we send people who have been prayed for to the clinic to be properly tested – so we can indeed verify that their healing is real and complete.

There cannot be many centres of ministry in the world that have clinics attached to them! Likewise, I am sure there are not many churches in the world that experience healing to the degree we do. If I was forced to answer the "Why?"

question, I would say that in the midst of tragedy God is always so real. It brings me back to the words I quoted earlier: "We only knew Jesus was all we needed when He was all we had left." Many Christians around the world who have suffered persecution testify to the fact that God was closest to them when their difficulties were at their most intense. God is faithful and He is always quick to intervene when His people are in dire need. We have very little here and are frequently in need – yet we constantly experience the glory of God's presence, His provision and His care. We know God is present with us through the visible activity of His Holy Spirit.

We may be in the fire but our God is also with us in the fire. He has been there before, for it was here, in what is now Iraq, that Shadrach, Meshach and Abednego were thrown into a blazing furnace. When King Nebuchadnezzar looked into the flames, he was astonished to see that there was a fourth person with them, who looked to him "like a son of the gods", and they were all walking around unharmed. Surely, this was the Lord. Today, too, we have seen that when our faith is being tested in the fire, the Lord is there with us – and this is true not only in Iraq but wherever we may be.

Love, forgiveness and perseverance

Every day, without fail, I pray the Lord's Prayer and so do most of my colleagues at St George's. We pray that God's will "be done on earth as it is in heaven". It is so easy to say these familiar words, but a lot more difficult to put them into practice – and yet it is essential. And this is not just a prayer for others, it is also a prayer for us. We need to know what the will of God is, and that means that we need to know what His nature is. We learn the latter primarily by examining the way that our Lord Jesus lived on earth.

When we study the life and teaching of Jesus in the Gospels, we see that He too lived "in the fire", and so He gave us a wonderful example of how we should live. For us at St George's, the things that really stand out are His love, forgiveness and perseverance. I have already referred to the first of these qualities in Chapter 3, but let me mention it again, because it is, along with the other qualities, what enables us to know that the Almighty is with us.

Love

Time and again in Baghdad we see that love is the answer. It is love that breaks down every barrier. It is love that has the power to transform darkness into light. All that we do – in the church, in the clinic, in my work outside St George's – is to demonstrate the love of Jesus. Most of our patients are not members of our congregation – indeed, most of them are Muslims – and when they ask why we give them free treatment, we tell them it is because of the love Jesus has for them. When we give out the groceries after church, we are clear that we do it because Jesus loves these people and wants to meet all their needs. We never forget the words of John the apostle: "God is love" (1 John 4:8).

Forgiveness

Flowing out of this love is the forgiveness that Jesus offers to all, and that we try to express in our lives. It is forgiveness not just for those we love but also for our enemies – the people who try to kill us, the people who do kill some of us, the people who have lit the fire that we live in. The forgiveness of Jesus is so radical and so all-consuming. It is the forgiveness that He expressed even from the cross as the soldiers crucified Him, saying, "Father, forgive them, for they do not know what they are doing" (Luke 23:34). We too are called to express a radical message of forgiveness to those who persecute us here in Baghdad.

Perseverance

It is Jesus' radical love and radical forgiveness that cause us to persevere. For us, taking up our cross and following Jesus is a literal, daily experience. I will talk more about this in the next chapter.

Despite our hardships, then, we know what it is to love, to forgive, and to persevere. Every week at St George's, when we say the creed together, we believe it. We do not doubt that God is to us everything He promises and more. We are assailed by many things, but not by doubt. We may have cried together, but together we have never doubted that God is with us. Even if we lose everything in earthly terms, we will never lose Him. Our God is constantly with us – and we are more aware of His presence than ever during our greatest difficulties.

10
MOVING FORWARD

Although I have stated previously that we can only live one day at a time here in Baghdad, I realize that we must still look forward. I may not know what even the next hour will bring, but as the leader of St George's I must also be a man of vision. This is true for all of us who are believers. We need to be people of vision who know where we are going. Our faith in Jesus is a faith which is always moving forward. When Jesus was ministering on the earth He was always on the move. So one thing that is never an option for us is going backwards.

What I find difficult as I try to determine the way forward, personally, is that it obliges me to stop and look at myself. I have to be willing to see myself as others see me. This is hard for me, for two reasons. First, it confronts me with the fact that many people see me as the person they want to destroy! I am the one they would like to see taken, dead or alive. Perhaps more difficult is the fact that others regard me as a hero, which I am not. I do appreciate the fact that God has given me very considerable influence here in Iraq, and I am privileged to have access to the most senior people in the nation at any time. I can call people together and they will respond. I am seen as someone who can make things happen and therefore people have high expectations of me. But I am constantly aware, however, that I can only do this under the direction of the Holy Spirit. I am who I am only by the grace of God, and I am here, doing what I'm doing, because God has sent me.

Nevertheless, I keep looking forward and hoping to move forward – despite the obstacles. One such obstacle is that of corruption in our nation of Iraq.

The problem of corruption

Much of my time over the years since the war in 2003 has been devoted to the problem of religious sectarianism. At one stage, all our efforts were focused on reducing violence and protecting minorities – for example, we put together the first ever fatwa against violence issued jointly by Sunni and Shia clerics – but now we have to devote a great deal of time to tackling corruption as well.

There is no way that the Iraqis can progress as a nation unless this issue is dealt with. This aspect of my work may not sound very holy, but it is very much directed by the Holy Spirit. Often the problem seems so great, so intractable, that we can only approach it under the direction of the Almighty. My prayer is simple: "Come, Holy Spirit! We need you."

Corruption permeates Iraqi society at every level. When the country was liberated in 2003, everyone here expected to become rich overnight. There is no sense that if you want to prosper you have to work very hard. Here, you don't make money, you take it. People will take (and take and take) at every level of society, from the government downwards. Demanding a bribe is regarded as almost legitimate, especially if the person you are demanding it from is not Iraqi – and so people will try to extract money from me at every opportunity. It is not possible just to say, "I'm sorry, we don't do that." Even to retrieve my luggage at the airport is difficult without paying somebody a backhander. I will be told that my bag has been impounded because something in it – usually, something such as medicine for the clinic – is not permitted; and if I don't pay the bribe they will summon their boss and he will back them up – and demand a further bribe himself. Then there are more people who want to take from you. It is so frustrating! Every time I arrive in Baghdad, I have to pray that this time I will get through without any trouble.

On the issue of corruption as much as on violence, I needed to invoke the help of some of Iraq's most senior religious figures, and recently we launched a Religious Leaders' Anti-Corruption Forum, which I shall direct. This whole side of our work has become much more complicated now that George W. Bush is no longer America's president, because we no longer have the funding we used to have and can no longer hold summit meetings outside Iraq. Many of the key Sunni religious leaders now live abroad, as it is far too dangerous for them to remain in Iraq, though their influence here is still just as strong. However, I still have to maintain my relationships with them all and so I regularly go and visit them.

The pursuit of peace

If we are to keep moving forward, we cannot do so without the direction of the Holy Spirit. Though I often find it difficult to see that we will ever achieve a fundamental peace here, we have to keep trying. If we pray for peace, then we have to work for it too. This is hugely time consuming, but necessary. Over the years I have been working in the Middle East, it has become clear to me that there are four major components that always form a part of the peacemaking process. I describe them as relationships, risk-taking, relief and reconciliation.

In my work of peacemaking, all four of these elements need to be fully implemented in order to move forward. Continually, I am having to ask myself how to move forward on various issues in light of the four Rs.

Relationships

Without the right substantive relationships, it is impossible to move forward. It is not simply a matter of knowing the right people; you have to become their friend. You need to spend time with these people, to listen to them and, if possible, share food with them. You cannot expect relationships here to develop quickly, as you might hope would be the case in the West. In the Middle East it can take months or even years to make friends with someone. I have found one way to speed up the process considerably, however, and that is by establishing that you have friends in common. This is true especially with religious leaders. If you can show them that you enjoy a warm relationship with other people who are friends of theirs, it is very likely that they, too, will embrace you as a friend. In

Iraq, there is a tribal element to this: come what may, you are always close to those of your own "tribe". Thus, as we think about how to make progress in our work of peacemaking, we are always thinking about how to maintain the relationships we have and how to invest in new ones.

Risk-taking

As my mentor, Lord Coggan, said to me: "Don't take care, take risks!" It is impossible to live one's life working on the front line without participating in risk-taking. Indeed, it is essential to our search for peace.

When we put together the High Council of Religious Leaders in Iraq, we decided that there were four types of people who had to be represented: those who have large religious followings, those who get a lot of media exposure, those who are well connected and influential politically, and those who are directly involved in the causes of the violence. It is obviously this last group that entailed the most risk – but it was clear to me that if you are working for peace, you have to work with those who are responsible for the violence and try to get them to stop. You can never break the downward spiral of violence only by working with nice people.

Of course, there are some that you cannot work with, such as al-Qa'ida. But whatever risks you are prepared to take, you still need to be totally reliant on the direction of the Holy Spirit – you cannot court danger just for the sake of it – and if you do not believe that the Spirit is urging you to do something, you do not do it. But when He leads you to take risks, in who you meet and where you meet them, and what you ask them to do for you, then you do it. There have been occasions when I and my colleagues have met people and the Iraqi authorities have been so fearful for our safety that they have hidden soldiers on the roofs around the building we were meeting in.

We have taken many risks in order to reduce violence in a particular place, and often they have borne fruit. Without taking risks we would not have formed crucial relationships and nothing would have changed. Much of the violence in Iraq is imported from outside. Groups such as al-Qa'ida are not Iraqi, though they may involve Iraqis. Their aim is to destroy "the other", whoever they may be: which means, as they are Sunni Arabs, they target Iraq's Shia majority as well as members of the Coalition and minorities such as the Kurds, the Christians, the Mandeans (who refer to themselves as the cousins of the Christians), the Yazidi (a group found predominantly in the north) and the Shabach (a large group of people thought to originate from Iran in the seventeenth century).

(There is also risk involved in our work against corruption. Some of the members of our Religious Leaders' Anti-Corruption Forum are fearful of reprisals from other Iraqis and have asked me whether I can provide them with security.)

Relief

Another essential in peacemaking is the provision of relief to those who are caught in the midst of the conflict, who often are suffering terribly as a result of injury or bereavement, unemployment or destitution. Often at the very heart of peacemaking is the need for those involved in the conflict to show that they can make a difference. For those who are hurting, help needs to be provided. But those doing the hurting also have needs to be met. Sometimes, meeting those needs is a necessary part of the process of turning them to peace. This is not optional – it is a must. True reconciliation can happen no other way.

Reconciliation

Once relationships, risk-taking and relief are in place, reconciliation begins to be a possibility – though there can never be any guarantees; there are no foolproof certainties in this work.

Every week, I am contacted by people wanting to know how I go about peacemaking. What is my methodology? A long time ago I would have had an answer to such questions. I knew all the theories; I knew what strategies other people had used and what they said worked. Now, I am more likely to tell you what does not work. I do know, however, that there can be no lasting peace without reconciliation, and no reconciliation without the other three Rs: serious, long-term relationships, a willingness to take enormous risks and the provision of real relief. For me there is one other factor that secular agencies cannot understand: the role of the Almighty in the process. The guidance and direction of the Holy Spirit in peacemaking can often cut to the heart of the most complex issues and find a way through. When on our own we cannot achieve anything, with Him all things become possible.

Making progress

I have often talked of what a wonderful church St George's is, and the extraordinary love and peace we enjoy there. But even there we need to move forward. We have our problems that need to be overcome. We have to think seriously about what we are doing and where we are going. And we have to keep planning ahead, even though we do not know even what the next hour will bring. All the time, we have to bear in mind that whatever we plan may come to nothing for reasons of "security" – because a bomb has gone off, or the roads have been closed, or someone has been killed.

Still the Lord keeps us moving forward and out of the ashes of devastation we see important progress. Recently, our lay pastor Faiz became the first Iraqi to be trained and ordained as an Anglican clergyman in his own country. He has served our church for a number of years and the leadership he has provided has been simply inspirational. His mother says that she had dreamed of this all her life and now it has happened! How grateful we are to our bishop for making this possible, but even more to our Lord, who answers our prayers and can make our dreams come true in ways that we never thought possible – not only in Iraq but wherever we happen to be in the world.

I have to make sure that I regularly spend time just listening to the Almighty, waiting for Him to tell me what to do next. One of the ways that He speaks to me is through other people, like my friend Jonathan Webb who suggested we open a clinic. At the time we had no funds to underwrite such a venture and no building to house it, but within two months we had a wonderful clinic with outstanding equipment and all the doctors and dentists and other staff we needed. I had been praying that God would show me a way to demonstrate the love of Jesus, but I never dreamed it could happen within our own compound. It is impossible in Baghdad to go out evangelizing – it would be a very quick way to die – but now people come to us.

The clinic has been seriously damaged by car bombs, and on one occasion was completely destroyed; but by God's grace it was totally restored in two months and in fact is even better than before. Such work is part of our way forward: a practical example, expressing the love of Jesus even in response to an attack. It is so hard to do sometimes, but the Lord always comes through in His magnificence. As I think about it, this must always be the way forward: taking risks to express the love of Jesus. This is the purpose of our clinic and also our kindergarten. This is why we provide our people with groceries every week. We move forward by seeking to meet the needs of those outside, as well as inside, the church.

As well as the physical needs of my congregation, I also have to think of people's spiritual needs and how we can equip them to live in the fire. Despite the fact that most of my people have been going to church all their lives, in the past they have been taught very little and so we spend a lot of time simply expounding the basics of what Christians believe. The Alpha course has been very helpful in this respect, and has been greatly appreciated. Even so, there are things that even the smallest members of my congregation can teach me. I will never forget the Christmas Day when I informed the children that I was going to tell them about Bethlehem, the place where I used to live, the place to which Jesus came first. A little boy put up his hand and said, "*Abuna, Abuna,* [Father, Father] Jesus did not go first to Bethlehem! He came here to Iraq – He was in the flames with Shadrach, Meshach and Abednego." I could not deny that he was right.

We know that Jesus existed before the foundation of the world. We know that He was involved in creation. Is it not amazing that the first time He appears to humankind is literally in a fire? Does that not tell us that even when we are in the fire, the Lord is with us in person, so that we are never alone? This is what I tell my people continually: we may be in the fire, but our Lord is there with us. It does not matter where we are physically, or what horrors we are suffering. Though the bullets may fly and the bombs explode, He is with us and by His grace He will help us to keep moving forward.

11

FRIENDS IN THE FIRE

Though the situation is hard in Baghdad, I am grateful to know that I am not here alone. The heavy security provided by the Iraqi government gives me a degree of protection, but nothing encourages me more than knowing there are those who are "with us" and supporting us either through their prayers, their finance, or both. I am grateful whenever I hear of organizations supporting the worldwide persecuted church, and personally we have been so thankful for the support of the global television network, GOD TV, and of my friend J. John's Philo Trust. Besides these friends, though, help from other organizations is pretty much non-existent and we could not survive without the support of many wonderful churches and individuals who give regularly.

People often ask how they can support us and I always reply, "Prayer and money!" As I write, a retired priest called David Pound is doing a sponsored cycle ride from his home in Lincolnshire all the way down to Land's End, and then the length of Britain up to John O'Groats, and then back home – a round trip of some 1,800 miles, and at the age of seventy-two! His T-shirt says simply, "St George's Baghdad". Here is a man who is serious about his support for the suffering church.

It is my hope that many more reading this, like David, will be moved to raise support for their brothers and sisters in Christ here in Iraq. To that end, I want to share with you the stories of some of those who have suffered or died for their faith. I could provide a very long list of people, but I will share the details of just a few, so far as we know them. Sometimes we do not even get the bodies of the dead back, and then it can be very difficult for their loved ones to accept that they are no longer alive.

The face of the suffering church

In *The Vicar of Baghdad*, I told how in 2005 our lay pastor Maher went to a Christian conference in Jordan with his wife, his fourteen-year-old son, his assistant and three others. On their way home we spoke by satellite phone as they crossed the border into Iraq and they told me what a good time they'd had. That was the last anybody heard of them. Maher left behind his daughter and his mother; the other members of their party did not have any children, but had been caring for elderly relatives. It was the first time we had had to take responsibility for people whose providers had been killed.

For two years thereafter I was in constant touch with relatives and friends of Maher and his family who could not believe that they were dead. A rumour quickly spread that they had been taken by the Americans and there were countless reports that they had been sighted in different jails. Every time I heard such a story I investigated it fully and invariably found that it was untrue, but no one wanted to believe what I had to tell them. It was such a painful experience. At times, I almost felt that I was being blamed for their disappearance. Curiously, I noticed that often relatives who had fled abroad many years ago found the loss harder to cope with than those who had stayed in Iraq. With so much bloodshed and destruction all around us, somehow death seemed easier for us to accept.

Another death that was very difficult to deal with was that of one of our guards, Bassam, who left a wife and three young children. We never really found out how he was killed, but it happened very near to the church and so we were able to retrieve his body. We paid for his funeral and to this day we provide for his family. Without our support, they have nothing. In my previous book, *Suffer the Children*,[3] his daughter Mariam wrote:

> *I am just a little girl from Baghdad. I used to have a wonderful, happy family ... until one day four years ago we heard [that my dad] had been killed. I was eight years old at the time and my dad was very important to me, and suddenly I could not play with him any more or call to him. I was so sad and desperate, because I had lost my dad forever. I had lost his face and his voice, I'd lost his presence in my life.*

Mariam's words bring home to us the stark reality of loss. Almost certainly, Bassam was killed because he was a Christian. He was part of our security team, but to me he was a friend.

---

3   Continuum, 2010.

He was a man of great faith and today he is in heaven.

Everyone at St George's now wears a bracelet, made for them by the young people of All Nations Church in Charlotte, North Carolina, that says simply "FRIENDS". It reminds them that they are friends both with each other and with God. One of our young men who was a policeman was caught with some colleagues in a terrible bomb attack, and all that was found of him was his hand, still with his bracelet around the wrist. We know that he was a friend of God and now he is with Him.

Several of our people have been killed merely because they were in the wrong place at the wrong time. Everybody in Iraq is at risk – not just the Christians for their faith. Everybody is hated as "the other" by someone else. In fact, the people who have suffered most are the Yazidi. So far, over a quarter of their number have been targeted and killed. Christians have taken the attacks on other minorities very seriously. The political leader of the Christians in the Iraqi parliament, Yonadam Kanna, has fought tirelessly for their protection and rights. It is a wonderful example of the way Christians care not just for our own, but for all who are suffering.

A vision of Jesus

I have already mentioned the eleven converts from Islam whom I baptized in secret last year, who were dead within a week. A little later, a man came to see me and told me that he, too, wanted to be a Christian. He had been coming to St George's for a while and, like everyone else who has come to me wanting to be baptized, he had a vision of Jesus telling him that this was what he had to do. (No one ever does any evangelism at our church. God does it all Himself.) This time, though, there was a serious complication, because this man was a prominent and highly respected sheikh who had many followers. I didn't want him to lose his life, so I told him that he needed to study the Bible with Faiz for six months and then let me know whether he still wanted to be baptized. I prayed for him – and as I did so, I had a vivid picture of the apostle Philip baptizing the Ethiopian eunuch (Acts 8:26–39). I realized that God wanted me to baptize him there and then, so I said "Amen" and without further ado baptized the sheikh there in my office. He cried as I did it. "It doesn't matter if I am killed," he told me. "All I want is to follow my Jesus." I am reminded of the inspirational words of the American missionary Elisabeth Elliot, whose husband lost his life in Ecuador: "Is the distinction between living for Christ and dying for Him, after all, so great? Is not the second the logical conclusion of the first?"

I learned so much from my new friend that day. He was going into the fire, but he knew that he had to follow Jesus and he wanted to; he knew that Jesus was the Lover of his soul. I told him not to tell anyone what had happened and he went on his way. He has taken huge risks for his faith, but he is still alive today. The only other people he has told that he is now a Christian are a few American soldiers – the ones who first sent him to me. He had had a difficult time at other churches in Baghdad when he went and told the priests that he wanted to follow Jesus. They were frightened of what might happen to them if they baptized a Muslim and agreed among themselves that they would not do it. However, I do not see how I can deter someone from following Jesus who wants to.

Countless people have been killed here, but it is the children who have died that I can never forget – the pain of it was just so unbearable. All they were guilty of was loving Jesus. Parents here constantly worry about their children. Some will not allow their children to go to school because they are afraid of what might happen to them. The fact is, schools here are targeted by terrorists and children certainly are at risk. Older girls are particularly vulnerable and numbers of them have been abducted, raped, and forced into Muslim conversion and marriage. Usually when this happens their parents never see them again.

In the safety of the Western world we talk about "suffering for Christ" but very few really know what it means. Even the worst attacks in a country such as Britain cannot be compared with what we see almost every day here in Iraq. I remember an occasion when I was walking down a street in south London, wearing my clerical collar. A Hare Krishna devotee came up to me and suddenly started to assault me, and even broke my glasses. I thought at the time that this was an appalling attack on me and my faith, but as I look back I now see that it was nothing. I used to read the Gospel accounts of the sufferings of many of the first Christians and think that they were so terrible, but now, I must confess, I do not think they compare with what my people here endure. The wider church needs to recognize that, despite not suffering in agony and terror themselves, we are all one family. Part of the family is hurting and the rest of the family needs to support it.

I remember how, a few years ago, before we really started

our relief work, people at St George's started asking me, "Don't the other Christians in the world care about us?" I told them the problem was that most Christians did not even know about them, which was a fact. I don't find it easy going around the world and speaking at different churches – I often long to be back with my own people – but I know that I have to do it to win support for St George's; and almost always I have found that the congregations I speak to have been very supportive.

I do not go to other churches only to ask for money; I also believe that other Christians need to hear our testimony. The apostle Paul sums up our experience in 2 Corinthians 4:16–18:

> *Therefore we do not lose heart. Though outwardly we are wasting away, yet inwardly we are being renewed day by day. For our light and momentary troubles are achieving for us an eternal glory that far outweighs them all. So we fix our eyes not on what is seen, but on what is unseen. For what is seen is temporary, but what is unseen is eternal.*

Even in the midst of the fire, my friends and I do not lose heart, for every sentence of this passage gives us hope. So often people ask me, "How can you be so happy when things are so awful?" The answer is here. Everything around us may be dreadful, we may be surrounded by violence and terror, we may seem to be wasting away, but we know that inwardly we are being renewed day by day. This is our constant experience. In truth, our Lord gives us the strength to keep going one day at a time. It is difficult for us to think beyond today, and I find it reassuring that Jesus Himself spoke about the importance of taking one day at a time. God's provision for His people in the wilderness came one day at a time (apart from the day before the Sabbath, when it was given for two). Yesterday's provision is no good for today.

So our Lord enables us to survive one day at a time and He renews us each day. We know that one day we will see God's glory in its fullness. I have said that we see His glory now in Iraq, but this is nothing compared with the glory that we shall see when we are with Him – a glory that we believe profoundly will only be the greater as a result of what we suffer now. If we thought that this suffering was permanent, it would crush us; but we know that it is not. These present troubles will last for a short while only, but what is to come hereafter will last forever. The pain may be terrible now, but we can endure it if we take one day at a time and look continually to the future, a heavenly future that is so real for us, as it should be for all Christians. We know that, as Paul says in Romans 8:18, "our present sufferings are not worth comparing with the glory that will be revealed in us."

12

THE REAL PRESENCE

I have said that at St George's we know God's presence in such a real way. I can talk about miracles and angels and wheels within wheels, but in truth the presence of God is seen most obviously in His people. The fact is that they are ordinary people doing extraordinary things in an extraordinary place. It is the Almighty who makes these people remarkable. It is His presence with them that makes them extraordinary. The words of Psalm 126 aptly describe the feelings of the believers here in Iraq:

> A song of ascents
>
> *When the Lord brought back the captives to Zion,*
> *we were like men who dreamed.*
> *Our mouths were filled with laughter,*
> *our tongues with songs of joy.*
> *Then it was said among the nations,*
> *"The Lord has done great things for them."*
> *The Lord has done great things for us,*
> *and we are filled with joy.*
>
> *Restore our fortunes, O Lord,*
> *like streams in the Negev.*

Those who sow in tears
will reap with songs of joy.
He who goes out weeping,
carrying seed to sow,
will return with songs of joy,
carrying sheaves with him.

Recently, I have been asking my congregation how the Lord helps them to survive. There are two very different answers that I receive, both of which could be summed up by words from the Psalms. Some people are very aware of the Lord's provision for them: like the writer of Psalm 126, they testify that they have sown the seeds that the love of God gave them and have come back carrying sheaves (though, unlike the psalmist, they may feel that they are still "in exile"). Others might quote a different Psalm, 137, which was written in what today is Iraq:

By the rivers of Babylon we sat and wept
when we remembered Zion.
There on the poplars
we hung our harps,
for there our captors asked us for songs,
our tormentors demanded songs of joy;
they said, "Sing us one of the songs of Zion!"

How can we sing the songs of the Lord
while in a foreign land?

I talk constantly about the wonderful people at St George's (and they all are wonderful), but there are some who "sit by the rivers of Babylon and weep" as they remember days past

– which were bad days, of course, but nothing compared to now. Today, there is no freedom in Iraq for Christians, nowhere where they can feel safe. "How can we sing the Lord's songs," they ask, "when we are in an alien land?"

We are certainly in an "alien land". Nothing here remotely approaches what could be regarded as normality – and yet we are continually looking for the presence of our Lord here in this strange place, and in the midst of its darkness and danger we still must sing the Lord's song. To a certain extent, it is an act of will: we have to decide to praise God, even when we find it difficult. I praise Him mainly in song, though I can't sing well; others praise Him with words of prayer.

God's community

To fully experience God's presence we do so not just as individuals, but through the lives of other believers. Yes, we can experience His presence for ourselves, but there is also a sense in which we must experience it corporately and as a community. We need to talk with others, pray with others, seek God with others, and listen to others and see what the Lord is saying to us through them. It is quite easy for me to relate to other people here and to engage with them, but for others it is much harder – not least because here men and women do not engage with each other. They do not even sit in the same pews in church: the men sit on one side of the aisle and the women on the other. There are two reasons for this tradition. First, it is part of the general culture here and most Iraqis would observe it; and second, it is what seems most proper to Christians.

We have had big discussions as to whether we can change things – especially in our youth services, where the two sexes are not allowed to mix in case they develop inappropriate relationships. On this score, I strongly disagree with their tradition. Of course, they are right to try hard to behave morally, but at times it can make communication very difficult and people need to engage with each other, especially in the house of God. In particular, it concerns me because the women seem to be so much closer to God and I want the men to learn from them. As their *Abuna* I can talk to anybody, male or female, young or old, and I hear the most amazing stories that I wish they could tell each other. This is one of the reasons why I ensure that we have a time in every service when people can talk about what has been happening to them – though it is a problem that a lot of people are afraid to speak in public.

To date, as many as four in five of Iraq's Christians have left the country because they have been attacked or threatened with attack; but perhaps half of those that remain have a clear understanding that their church is the house of God and do not want to leave it. Some of our congregation leave, but people are still coming in their thousands. These are the ones who are so aware of the presence of God – and indeed are a manifestation of the presence of God. They have no doubt that God is with them in Iraq and has plans for their nation. They regard what the church gives them as God's gift to them. The food, the health care; these are seen as the Lord's provision for them "according to his glorious riches in Christ Jesus" (Philippians 4:19). Each week as people collect their groceries, I see them lift up their hands to heaven in thanks to the Almighty.

The people of Iraq have suffered a great deal, and in the past, many say, they blamed God. Many still do – but very few of my people. In fact, I have to say, I have never met anyone at St George's who does. We are a positive community and the attitude of the group affects the individual. That is not to say that my people find things easy – there is nothing easy about living in the fire in one of the most dangerous places in the world! However, together we can be aware of the presence of Almighty God with us – we have seen Him at work so often. We have seen His miracles, we have seen His angels – but nothing seems as real as His presence. We see Him in each other's eyes, we hear Him speaking to us, as He did to Elijah, in "a gentle whisper" (1 Kings 19:12). Even if there were no miracles or angels we would know that what we say at the beginning of each service is true: "*Allah hu ma'na wa Ruh al-Qudus ma'na aithan.*" ("God is here, and His Holy Spirit is here.")

The question God whispered to Elijah at the mouth of his cave was: What are you doing here? This is a question that people here regularly ask and discuss. What are we doing here? We are waiting for God to intervene. Wherever I go outside Iraq, people ask me why I am here. The answer is always the same: I am where I know God has called me to be, doing what I know He has called me to do. My people, too, are where God has called them to be.

As I walk into St George's each day, I pass a picture of Elijah sitting by the cave with the raven. It always reminds me that the voice of God is often "still" and "small", a gentle whisper. The Almighty does not speak to us only in large and dramatic ways – this is why we always have to listen closely to Him each day. How do we catch God's gentle whisper? There is no simple answer to this. We have to learn to listen to the voice of God within us, which comes to our minds directly. It has taken me a long time to learn to recognize it. I know that it will never contradict what we read in the Bible or go against the fundamentals of our faith and practice; but still it is not always easy to hear accurately. I have said that there are always risks involved in the kind of work I do and one of those risks is hearing God correctly and acting on what He says. Sometimes I make a mistake because I mishear Him. Yet, the more we listen, the more likely we are to know what God is saying in that gentle whisper.

Holy Communion

We also experience the real presence of God through Holy Communion – which is something a person from my tradition would not normally say; usually it is Catholics who talk about the "real presence" in the Eucharist. But then at St George's we rejoice in our immense diversity. In my congregation we have Orthodox, Chaldeans, Catholics, Assyrians, Evangelicals and Charismatics. Essentially we are Anglicans and open to every tradition (though we are very firm about the non-negotiable truths of our Christian faith).

In the Anglican Church, the understanding of Holy Communion is very much in line with what the Church Father Thomas Aquinas taught. Like the name of God in the Hebrew scriptures, it is past, present and future. In Latin, it is said to be held:

* *Respectu præteriti*, (in respect of the past) – it is a commemoration of the sacrifice of our Lord in His Passion on the cross.
* *Respectu presentis*, (in respect of the present) – it unites the church as a body. This is why we call it "Holy Communion", because in this act of worship we are communicating with Christ and partaking in the very emblems of his Deity.
* *Respectu futuri*, (in respect of that which is to come) – it is a "prefiguration" of what it will be like to be with our Lord in heaven, when we will see His face and be like Him.

The sacrament is also called the "Eucharist", which is equivalent to the Latin *bona gratia*, (good grace), because eternal life is the grace of God, or else because it is seen as representing Christ, who is full of grace.

It may sound like complex theology, but in truth this is what I am thinking when I celebrate Holy Communion. We may be in the fire – or the crossfire (even as I write these words, I can hear rockets flying: there is a major Shia festival going on and the Sunna do not like it!) – but we know that we are not alone: the Lord is here with us, revealing Himself in the miraculous and the angelic, talking to us in a gentle whisper and meeting us in the Eucharist, and we have each other.

Almost no one at St George's is an Anglican by tradition, but when I ask my people why they come to a church that is not part of their denomination they tell me frankly that originally they came because they heard that we gave out groceries. But then they all say that they learned what the church was really like, and that "God is here". They tell me that now they will never leave St George's, even if we stop giving them food, because they have seen how God protects this place, how He meets with them here, speaks to them through miracles, visions and dreams, and meets them in Holy Communion. Ultimately, though, they say they have experienced the presence of God in the love that fills this place: the love we show each other, the love that drives out all fear – God's love that never ceases. As we read in the Hebrew scriptures, in Lamentations 3:22–24 (in the ESV):

> *The steadfast love of the Lord never ceases;*
> *his mercies never come to an end;*
> *they are new every morning;*
> *great is your faithfulness.*
> *"The Lord is my portion," says my soul,*
> *"therefore I will hope in him."*

I may be under immense fire, as are my people, but our hope is indeed in Him and therefore we do not fear.

Epilogue

The Massacre at the Church of Our Lady
of Deliverance in Baghdad

It was Sunday 31 October 2010 and many people were in church for the main service of the day. Most of our people were worshipping at St George's, but some were visiting the Syrian Catholic church situated very close by. There the Bible reading had taken place and the sermon was about to begin when the Catholic church was invaded by nine al-Qa'ida terrorists. They shot people dead, scattered grenades and finally blew many people up with a suicide bomb. Most of the details of this event are too awful to mention, but in all fifty-eight people were killed. It was the worst massacre of Christians in Iraq for many years.

I didn't know whether people would dare to return to church the following week – they were so frightened. The massacre caused widespread fear as people realized how poor their security situation was and how uncertain their future was. Many wanted to leave. As ever, many were determined to stay, but their number has decreased. In the last few weeks our congregation has fallen by around 500 people to 3,500. Many have fled to Syria and have sought the support of the Anglican church there, hoping to receive the same kind of support as they did from St George's. But the Syrian church is not able to help them and, once they leave Iraq, sadly neither can we.

The week after this tragedy I spoke on Romans 8:18–21:

> *I consider that our present sufferings are not worth comparing with the glory that will be revealed in us. For the creation waits in eager expectation for the children of God to be revealed. For the creation was subjected to frustration, not by its own choice, but by the will of the one who subjected it, in hope that the creation itself will be liberated from its bondage to decay and brought into the freedom and glory of the children of God.*

After preaching I listened to what our people had to say and heard many stories about what had happened to them during the week. The question many of our young people had was simply, "Why has all this happened to us? Why has God not stopped it?" There are no simple answers to these questions. Paul's words in Romans are the nearest thing we have to a response. We really do suffer with Christ, but we really do see His glory. We know that whatever happens, the Lord will sustain us and help us through our difficulties. The resounding message from our congregation was that they would not be deterred by the threats and intimidation because Jesus was still with them. They were unhappy with those who said that Iraqi Christians should leave Iraq, including the French government, who were offering asylum for 150 families. Despite the terrible things that have happened, they (and I) have resolved to stay. We know that "the Lord is here and His Spirit is with us."

CONCLUSION

My hope in writing this book is that it will awaken many to the immense suffering and pain of Iraq and of those here who call Jesus their Lord. Christians are being targeted here and the country as a whole continues to suffer the problems caused by the war over many years. Immense health problems are suffered by the masses. There is not a single community that has not been persecuted by others.

Under Saddam's regime things were very different. People often say that it was safe for the Christians in those days. It was certainly a lot safer. Saddam was a Sunni, who are a minority, so his regime was kinder to other minorities, including Christians, since he wanted to keep their support. In those days the most persecuted were not the minorities, but the majority Shia. What they endured was terrible. The other group that suffered terribly was the Kurds. They were terrorized en masse. And of particular significance was the onslaught against Halabja, when thousands were killed by chemical weapons.

Yet, we are not in despair. I cannot speak for the other churches in this land, but I can speak for St George's. We now

153

have the largest church in Iraq – a church which had nobody in it in 2003. We have so many people now, in fact, that it is impossible to fit them all in the building. People have flocked here because they have discovered God's presence and have witnessed His glory as never before. We do not escape the terrible suffering of this place – far from it, we are so often under fire – but we have faith and purpose and the presence of the Almighty to sustain us. The experience of His presence is more real to us than anything else.

Today my work is very diverse. Much of it is not church work, but political and diplomatic. It holds many challenges – corruption, terrorism, nepotism, religious sectarianism and much more. We see the effects of "religion" here – religion that has gone very wrong and has reached a state that is hard for most to comprehend. I simply wait on the Holy Spirit to bring about change. One of the difficulties of this type of work is that I find myself dealing one day with angry religious leaders and the next day with US diplomats representing the Coalition. The approach required to deal with each could scarcely be more different – disorganized Arab culture on the one hand and meticulously arranged American red tape on the other. The Coalition leaders expect results now, while with the Iraqis one must be patient and wait, wait, wait. The two groups have just one thing in common – neither really understands the spiritual dynamics of living out one's faith under fire.

Despite this lack of understanding there is always a concern for the persecution of minorities and the targeting of Christians. That said, there is frequently little understanding of how it might be dealt with effectively or how to stop those who are doing the targeting. There is never any guarantee of any initiative being successful. Things can be done to try to bring about change, but the danger can never be stopped. One very positive thing about our relationship with the Coalition is that the Anglican/Episcopal Chapel at the US Embassy and St George's Church see themselves as one congregation. We have one church council and every week we take a small number of Iraqi members to the US Embassy service. They care about us. They know the danger that we continually face and we know they are our brothers and sisters. Even though they are also under threat, they know that life for us is very different from their life in the Green Zone.

Recently, as I talked to the Mothers' Union here, I asked them how they manage to keep going when there is so much against them. Their answer was simple: "As we do the work of the Lord, He always comes with us." Jesus Himself is their only hope and assurance. A short time ago I accompanied these ladies as they visited the Sisters of Charity home for severely congenitally disabled children. We travelled through Baghdad with the protection of my security. I first visited here twelve years ago. The children here with missing arms and legs are the product of a broken society. Many people say they were born this way because of the toxic chemicals released during the war. Most of these children were born as Muslims, but it is the Christians who care for them and they are raised as Christians. This is not acceptable to Islam, but nobody else will care for them. Here, these defenceless children, who can do little more than speak, sing hymns with us, proclaiming their love for Jesus.

Those who care for them are also at risk, but they belong

to a community that is dedicated to serving those who have nothing. The love of this place truly sums up for me what serving our Lord here is all about.

Led into the fire

This book is only of significance if it can change our perception of suffering, and I pray that it has done so for you. It reminds us that in many places in the world, not just in Iraq, there are brothers and sisters of ours who are suffering for their faith. But, surprisingly, those same brothers and sisters have much to teach us about joy and experiencing the fullness of the presence of God. They teach us that we all, regardless of the circumstances in which we live out our faith, must pursue the presence of Jesus, so that His love can sustain and enable us.

Meanwhile, we remain here in Iraq. God gives us the ability to wait and see a difference in this nation. There may indeed be tears at night, but joy will come in the morning. This is indeed a place of God's glory, a place where wonderful things are happening, a place that is vitally connected to the last days.

I am indeed living under fire here, as are all the people of Iraq, but there is one difference: I chose to be here. I wasn't born here or sent here on a tour of duty – I chose to come. As I have said before, my understanding is that I have been sent here by the Almighty. I have also said many times before that I love it here and have no desire to leave. The Lord has given me a deep love for this place and this people.

I had no idea when I was ordained that I would end up working for peace in Iraq, and I had no desire to do so; but the Lord provided all that was needed and then gave me the desire. He didn't just provide for me either, but for my wife and my children as well. So, I accept now that I am under fire – but so will we all be at some time in our lives. It may not involve bullets, rockets or bombs, but we will all experience opposition and spiritual attack.

This, then, is why today I find myself in the fire. I never had any intention of entering it: it is simply where I was led. I can say that everything I have done in my life has brought me to this place, and God is here with me. I frequently hear people in church using the expression, "for such a time as this". Well, I am in this place for this time. This is, as I often say, the best job I have ever had.

Our story and song

The words of the prophet Habakkuk resonate strongly with the people of Iraq. In the opening verse of his prophetic book he cries out in frustration at the devastation he sees in the nation:

> *How long, O Lord, must I call for help,*
> *but you do not listen?*
> *Or cry out to you, "Violence!"*
> *but you do not save?*
> *Why do you make me look at injustice?*
> *Why do you tolerate wrong?*
> *Destruction and violence are before me;*
> *there is strife, and conflict abounds.*

Habakkuk 1:2–3

Habakkuk's experience is mirrored by the experience of multitudes here in Baghdad. And, like Habakkuk, it is easy to become angry at the situation. Yet, despite our intense frustration, we know that God is not silent and is not unaware of our situation. God had an answer for Habakkuk and His answer is the same for us:

> *Look at the nations and watch —*
> *and be utterly amazed.*
> *For I am going to do something in your days*
> *that you would not believe,*
> *even if you were told.*
>
> Habakkuk 1:5

In the end, the prophet is forced to stand back in total awe of his God and say:

> *Lord, I have heard of your fame;*
> *I stand in awe of your deeds, O Lord.*
> *Renew them in our day,*
> *in our time make them known;*
> *in wrath remember mercy.*
>
> Habakkuk 3:2

And then we read in Habakkuk 3:17–18:

> *Though the fig-tree does not bud*
> *and there are no grapes on the vines,*
> *though the olive crop fails*
> *and the fields produce no food,*
> *though there are no sheep in the pen*

and no cattle in the stalls,
yet I will rejoice in the Lord,
I will be joyful in God my Saviour.

Habakkuk learned, as we have had to learn, that despite so much being wrong with the world around us, despite having nothing, God is still everything. Despite our suffering we are not miserable, but joyful! I am privileged to lead the happiest church I have ever known and the joy of the Lord gives me strength.

I have been shot at, held at gunpoint, kidnapped, and had "Wanted" posters put up all over Baghdad offering huge sums of money in return for my capture. The heat of the fire is intense here, but so is the joy of the Lord.

This is my story, this is my song,
Praising my Saviour all the day long.[4]

---

4   Fanny Crosby, "Blessed Assurance".